This book was practical, frank, real ....
The chapters related to the new widow's support of
children was particularly insightful. I have seen many
children in my juvenile courts as a result of self
destructive behavior stemming from the death of a parent.
This book examines how to let your children grieve and
grow with you. This book is a must read for new
widows, especially those with small children.

Dana D. Huffman
Municipal Court Judge and Prosecutor

This book is very successful in its focus, setting out a course
of action   **Date: 9/2/11**   le
resource
paralysi   **306.882 BOY**
events.   **Boyanton, Janet.**
stories k   **Alone and alive :**
reading. _____ idices
assist us in getting our lives on track, from bill payment
to retirement and funeral planning. The last section, a
booklet the author offers to her clients, should be in
everyone's Will folder, completed, so that family and
friends have guidance in end-of-life planning. This is a
book to keep on the shelf, and to give to friends for
guidance.

Nancy F. Tiegreen
'ster

Alone and Alive is Janet Boyanton, Esq.'s "practical guide for dealing with the death of your husband". The common refrain that you will read begins, "Wait at least a year before [insert next piece of advice].

I have seen the wisdom and outcome of implementing these things in her life and the life of her son. Perhaps the best thing about the book is that nine years later, she is alone, alive and succeeding, as is her son. The cliché might be "the proof is in the pudding".

The book is simple, straightforward and easy-to-understand. She heightens the awareness of the friends and acquaintances who will make the process harder than it should be.

The "Decision Making Worksheets" at the end of the book cause you to focus on things that you may not have considered. If you have experienced the recent death of a parent, then this book may provide the impetus to get your own affairs in order.

Janet Boyanton has waited nine years to write this guide. What she has lived and learned is valuable for all of us.

Ralph J. Turner, MD FACOG
Assistant Professor of Surgery
University of Texas Health Science Center
at Tyler
Tyler, TX 75708

Being a new (less than a year) widow, I found the book to be very helpful. It was straightforward and easy to follow and understand. The experiences that she faced at the beginning were very familiar to me. For a woman who finds themselves alone (not having family near-by or easily available) the information in the book would be a wonderful guide as to what to expect and how to handle it.

Tracy Huffman, Recent Widow

A book that certainly speaks from the heart and provides an insightful perspective for continuing life after the loss of a loved one. We get to view this process through the author's own personal experiences. What's surprising is that this book is so easy to read, yet we still find great advice about how to solve legal and financial problems

Fred Hepner
Attorney at Law & Certified Public
Accountant

It is an honor to review this poignant and personal guide for dealing with the death of a husband. As Ms. Boyanton's personal Physician for many years I have been privileged to participate in many of her life's joys and sorrows, including the planning and delivery of her son and the death of her husband. I have watched her face and emerge from all these experiences a stronger and more determined person. She is well qualified to author this compelling guide based on her own life-changing experiences. The book provides a candid and reassuring emotional guide for this trying time. It also addresses the practical aspects and offers guidelines for preparing for these events. Altogether a must read!

Stacy R. Stephens, M.D.

Janet Boyanton, Esq. has written an excellent analysis of the psycho-social, financial and legal matters related to widowhood. She generously portrays her own loss with the death of her husband. It describes the wrong advice of others, the mistakes in decisions as well as the eventual lessons learned. The legal worksheets are a true benefit and put most issues into perspective. This fast read and thoughtful analysis reflects the grief and reconciliation process on the road to a "new Normal".

Charlotte M. Maxim, LMSW
Home Health Social Worker

Alone and Alive delivers critical information for the widow at the most vulnerable time of her life. As a recent widow, I encourage every widow to read this book. It contains concise information throughout and helpful worksheets in the appendix which will guide them through a mound of necessary decisions.

Sarah Lack
Associate Director of Transfer Students at
Northwood University-Texas Campus
2003 Best Southwest Leadership Class

Every woman, married, single or widowed should read this book, and most men should, too. It tells you how to prepare for and deal with the many decisions encountered following a death.

Pat Carpenter
Widowed Twice

"The journey of a thousand miles begins with a single step." *An Old Chinese Proverb*

Janet Boyanton's book, Alone and Alive, is a must read for any woman walking the path of surviving the loss of a spouse and those beginning the long journey of a *thousand miles.*

Janet's writing style and engaging manner of sharing the intricacies of her own deeply personal journey, losing her husband and father of her young son, at the age of 46, caught the heart of this reader from the beginning of the book until the very last page. Drawing on her own experiences, she shares a plethora of time-tested, wise and helpful insights, delving deeper into the myriad of details that must be handled during the aftermath of such a deep and personal loss.

Providing excellent "*reality based, in the moment and new normal*" tools and invaluable resources for a widow, Janet presents a seasoned narrative into the personal aspects of *growing through* mourning and grief. She chooses and uses her words brilliantly and applies her efficient understanding and legal expertise as an attorney, providing clarity and unique solutions to women challenged by the death and loss of their spouse.

Janet writes her heart from the perspective of a woman who has learned to pick up the pieces of her own life, as a young widow and mother, and today, carries on the life of her family with dignity and strength.

Bravo, Janet, for your courage and determination in sharing your heartfelt story and for your lasting gift in touching the lives of so many precious women who will read this book and walk the long journey beside you!

Marti Miller, ADC
Professional Speaker. Performer. Trainer and Developer.
Praise Leadership Training and Development
www.praiseleadership.com

Alone and Alive

A practical guide for dealing with

the death of your husband

By

Janet Boyanton, Esq.

aloneandalive.com

Cover Design by DHL Creative

Shafer Publishing is registered in Somerset County, New Jersey

Shafer Publishing, PO Box 134, Lyons, NJ 07939. Phone: (908) 432-1206.   ShaferPublishing.com

Library of Congress Control Number : 2011927115

ISBN: 9780974772028

Printed in the United States of America
May, 2011
First Edition

This book is dedicated to

Thomas Boyanton, my son. It has been a joy watching him grow into a wonderful young man.

And

The memory of
Robert Earl Boyanton, my husband.

March 28, 1949 - August 10, 2001

Acknowledgment

First I want to thank my son Thomas, who suffered with me through the writing of this book. He has been a constant source of encouragement and I thank him for that.

I would like to thank my secretaries Linda Sharp and Cathy Henderson who typed multiple drafts, proofread and advised through the book. I have no doubt this book would never have made it onto paper without them.

I would like to thank my initial proof reader Carolyn Clayton for her hard work and carefully thought out suggestions.

Also, Jodi Hendon my editor/proofreader, who worked hard to make sure I didn't make too many huge grammatical mistakes. She offered valuable advice which helped provide a more readable book.

I would like to thank my publisher, Julie Ciuro of Shafer Publishing, for believing in my work and making it become real.

And, finally, I would like to thank Steve Hendon, my business coach, (http://practicetobusiness.com) for his constant encouragement, helpful insights, occasional prodding, and confidence in my ability to write this book. Without his help I am certain this book would still just be an idea.

Contents

xi

CHAPTER 1

When the World Turned Upside Down:

The Day You Became a Widow

> You may be alone, but you are very much alive.
> Becoming a widow does not end your life. It simply
> begins a new phase.

This book will not be about sadness. It is not the tear-jerking story of a grieving widow. It is the story of how to overcome the grief and recapture the joy of life. It's the story of how you live in your newfound state, how you move on, and most important, how you stay yourself, even when you feel like part of you is gone forever.

<u>MY STORY</u>

My world turned upside down on August 10, 2001. Bob, my husband, Thomas, our nine-year-old son, and I had returned from vacation in Ireland and Scotland just three weeks earlier. It was a great trip, a nearly perfect family vacation. But I didn't realize it would be the last vacation we would all have together.

That fateful morning in August began innocently enough. It was Friday, and Bob had taken the day off from work to go camping with Thomas at a nearby lake. The trip was a celebration of Thomas's tenth birthday the following Monday. As I dressed for work, Bob came in from packing the tents and told me he and Thomas wanted to take me to breakfast that morning. I hesitated, thinking of the hectic day I had scheduled at work. My private law practice was booming, and I was very busy. In the end, I decided that I could take a few minutes to meet them at Braum's, which was on my way to work.

We had a quick breakfast. It was just an ordinary breakfast, on an ordinary day. We laughed and Thomas talked excitedly about what they were going to do at the lake. They had big plans for the day, swimming, hiking, and bicycling. I ate quickly, and headed out to my car. I realized I had the vacuum cleaner in my car, so I grabbed it to put in Bob's truck. Just then, Bob, who had seen what I was doing, appeared at my elbow, and, taking the vacuum cleaner from me, promised to drop it at the house before going to the lake. He then kissed me good-bye, with a fond "I love you" and "have a good day." I drove away, confident that the next morning I would see him return home from the lake. That wasn't going to happen.

He called me during the day to chat and tell me what they were doing. That was a normal part of our routine when somebody was out of pocket. He and Thomas were having a great time. Around 5:00, I got a call inviting me to come out and eat hot dogs with them for dinner. I passed on the hot dogs. Bob laughed, knowing that I would not come, and I knew the invitation wasn't serious. I said goodbye to him and headed to the house.

I was looking forward to my evening alone, and I had plans to watch a movie. When I got home, I noticed a call from Bob on the caller ID just minutes before I arrived. I dialed him back, but his cell phone was busy. I hung up and muttered something about people calling and then turning off their cell phone. As I turned to walk away, the phone rang. I picked up and heard my son's voice.

The sound of Thomas's voice filled me with dread. "Mom, Dad is sitting in a chair with his eyes closed, and he won't open them, even if I yell at him." I knew instantly what had happened. I told Thomas that I would call for an ambulance. I asked him if there were any adults around. "No," he said. I told him to stay with his dad, keep the phone where he could answer it, and that I would call him back. I needed to hang up and get an ambulance to help his dad, I told my distressed, but amazingly calm, nine-year-old.

I called for the ambulance, and gave the dispatcher Bob's cell phone number. They would call Thomas to find out where they were camping in the park. I had failed to get that crucial piece of information. I called Thomas back and told him the ambulance was on the way. I located my brother and, miraculously, he was close by the entrance to the state park, though he lived nowhere near it. He and his wife immediately went to the park, so Thomas wouldn't be alone.

Jumping in my car, I headed toward the park also. Halfway there the police dispatcher got hold of me. "Don't go to the park," she said. I was to go to the hospital and wait. Also, she asked permission to release Thomas to my brother. I assured her that was fine. There were so many details to deal with in the middle of the crisis.

I drove to the hospital, but when I arrived the ambulance wasn't there. I was disturbed by this, because the park was closer to the hospital than I was. I paced and waited, and still no ambulance. Fifteen, twenty, thirty minutes I waited, checking periodically with the nursing staff. No, I was told, the ambulance had not come in, but they knew it was coming. Finally, one of the nurses asked me for information. But rather than filling out the triage form, they took me behind the nurse's desk, offered me a seat, typed the information directly into the computer, then offered to get me coffee, tea, a cold drink, anything I wanted. I had the feeling that they knew what I already suspected, that Bob was dead.

When they cleared out the private family room and put me in there, I knew that the news was bad. Finally, thirty-five minutes after the original call, the ambulance pulled in. I raced out to meet it. As the doors opened, I saw my husband in his swim trunks, with an automated CPR machine pounding his chest. A nurse pulled at me to try to move me away from the scene, but I had to stand and watch. I needed to see Bob. Only after he was in the treatment area did I move back to the family room. Then Thomas arrived.

Now my wait was short. Only a few moments after Bob's arrival, a doctor came in and told us that Bob could not be resuscitated and she needed to stop trying. It was over. In the span of less than an hour, my life had changed forever.

FIRST COMES THE GRIEVING

This book will not be about sadness. It is not the tear-jerking story of a grieving widow. It is the story of how to overcome the grief and recapture the joy of life. It's the story of how you live in your newfound state, how you move on, and most important, how you stay yourself, even when you feel like part of you is gone forever.

After struggling through the decisions, events, and emotions that followed in the weeks and months after my husband's death, I realized that there was no guide to help the new widow. Certainly, there are many good books on grief, and grief books are very beneficial, but the things a new widow needs to know go well beyond dealing with grief. This book will address not only the issues of grief, but also many other issues that are commonly faced after the death of a spouse.

Topics to be discussed include:

- Help from friends and family
- Where to live - alone or with relatives
- Retirement home or roommate?
- Assessing your new financial realities
- Probate and other estate matters
- Keeping or selling your house
- Helping your children (of all ages) deal with the death

- Re-planning your legal affairs
- Dealing with "stuff"
- Hiring repairmen or do-it-yourself
- Forgiving yourself
- Your new daily routine
- Loving yourself

In addition, this book will look at the changes in your life and social status, from being part of a couple to a woman alone, and how that impacts your life. It will also address more mundane problems, like how to pick a repairman and how to deal with your new financial reality.

I am not a psychiatrist, therapist or grief counselor, though I deal with the effects of grief often in my law practice. I have counseled many widows, and other grieving family members, on the effects of grief and the life transitions that follow.

While my experience as a lawyer, my Master's of Business Administration, and my Master's of Divinity give me the tools necessary to help the new widow, my personal experience has given me insights my education never could.

Mostly I am a widow like you. I have walked this road and emerged whole. This book is a melding of my personal experiences, the experiences of the many widows I have worked with, and my training to provide practical information for the new widow.

In short, my hope is that this guide will provide you with some nuts and bolts information and resources to survive the transition into widowhood and emerge whole and happy. You may be alone, but you are very much alive. Becoming a widow does not end your life. It simply begins a new phase. The transition is not easy or pleasant, but it is possible to come through it and step out on the other side alive, vibrant, and ready to embrace your new life as a woman alone.

CHOICES

The grieving widow is at a crossroad. She can choose to wrap herself in her grief and live there permanently, becoming prematurely old and bitter. She can embrace self-pity, shrinking from the demands of her new situation and becoming totally dependent on the help of others. Or she can fearlessly accept and deal with the death of her husband. Only by dealing with the grief can she stay herself and experience joy once again.

For each of us this is the challenge. This book will provide you with some of the information you need to help you on your journey to joy.

CHAPTER II

Friends and Family

Helpful or Harmful

Wait a year before making life-changing decisions. This is
the first piece of advice I give to new widows.

Your world has turned upside down. You are
unsure as to how to proceed, but you may rest assured
that there are dozens of well-meaning friends and family
ready to offer you assistance, and not surprisingly, advice
on what you should do.

MY STORY

Immediately after my husband's death, even
before the funeral, I had people asking me if I was going
to sell his truck. Was I interested in getting rid of his
tools, they wanted to know. Surely, I was going to sell
the house. After all, the house was too big for me, they
opined. A number of well-meaning friends suggested
that I should shut my private practice and stay home with
my child (who was in fourth grade), or conversely, I
should close my private law practice and go look for a
"real" job? (I have often wondered what they thought I
was doing all those years, playing lawyer, perhaps?)

8

Everybody had an opinion on what I should do. I found myself in the rather awkward position of having to politely ignore the well-meaning advice of family and friends and follow the advice I had given to widows over the years as a probate attorney. I also found that I preferred giving the advice, rather than having to follow it.

WAIT AT LEAST A YEAR BEFORE MAKING LIFE-ALTERING DECISIONS

Unless there is a compelling reason for making a major life change, (i.e. you can't afford to pay for your house; you have to move somewhere you have child care available, etc.) you should wait at least a year to make life altering decisions. This is one of the first pieces of practical advice I give to new widows. It is nearly always best to wait a minimum of a year before making major decisions, such as selling the house, moving to a new location, changing jobs, shutting your law practice, etc., because your decisions are often driven by extreme emotion, not rational thought. Decisions made during this time period will not always be the best decisions for your future. People are standing by, ready to give you advice on anything and everything, but in the pain and emotional distress following the death of a spouse, the grieving widow is not really in a position to make the best decisions.

Immediately after death there is so much emotional pain that it is difficult to see the future, much less make rational plans for a future you cannot even imagine. For months after the death your decisions will be driven by grief, fear, and pain, not by what will be best for your future.

Selling the family home often seems like a good idea, because it is filled with memories of your spouse. You see your husband's clothes. You look at the spot where he slept on the bed. You see where he always sat to watch TV. You handle the remote, and you can almost feel him still touching it. Everywhere you look there are painful reminders of a life you no longer have. The urge to run away from painful memories can cause you to do things you will later regret.

A friend of mine lost his wife following a brief fight with cancer. He was devastated. For months he slept on the couch. The bed where they had slept together was simply too hard to bear. He could see where she slept, and for a time could smell her scent on the sheets. The memories of wonderful times that were gone forever was too painful in the months following her death.

Changing homes in the heat of emotion can have several, significant consequences. The most obvious is that later you will regret having walked away from the memories; but a second less obvious consequence is that selling your house and moving may ultimately create severe financial hardship. In your urgency to escape the painful memories or to find a new "happy" life, you may make business decisions driven by that sense of urgency and not by good judgment. You may lose money on the sale. You may find yourself with a larger mortgage on your new house, a higher interest rate than your current mortgage, and a longer payment period. You could be throwing away money that you need to secure your future.

Relocating to live in a retirement center or with family members may leave you isolated from friends and support systems. You may later find that you would have preferred to live alone. Unfortunately, that option may no longer be available and you may be forced to settle for a less than ideal living arrangement.

Moving involves disposing of a great many personal items. This can cause you to get rid of things because they are too painful to look at, because you won't have room for them, or because it is easier not to deal with the pain of sorting through the possessions of a lifetime together. Later you may regret your choices and you can never retrieve those items.

Changing jobs, churches, or social groups to escape from the memories of being a couple can leave you isolated and without a support system when you need it most. This isolation can occur even while living with your family or surrounded by new people at church or work. This is a time to be surrounded by people who know you and care about you. It is not the best time for making lasting new friendships.

During your initial grief and the long recovery that follows, you need to be surrounded by people who know you and really care about you. I was fortunate that my close friends at church allowed me to grieve and recover at my own pace. When I was sad, they accepted me as sad. When I felt like doing things, they took that as ordinary, but they never pushed me to move faster than I could.

Decisions that should not be made too quickly following the death of a spouse include:

- Selling your home
- Moving to a retirement center
- Moving in with relatives
- Moving relatives into your home to "help"
- Changing jobs
- Changing churches
- Stopping social activities with your couple friends
- Allowing someone to take over your finances
- Throwing out everything that makes you sad

DON'T GET RID OF HIS STUFF UNTIL YOU ARE READY

People will want to come in and carry off your husband's clothes, his shaving equipment, his athletic equipment, his tools, etc. Resist the urge to allow people to do that. While it is their intent to take away the things that produce painful memories and make it easier for you, the reality is they often injure your grief process instead of helping.

As much as you don't like it, going through your spouse's clothing, his toiletries, and other personal items, can be a helpful experience. It helps you come to terms with finality of his death. It brings back good memories of times when you were a couple.

Everyone is ready to deal with possessions at a different time. There is no set time or program for your grief. Each person is unique and ready to move forward when it feels right. Your husband's clothes do not have to be sorted and out of the house in two weeks. They do not have to be gone in two years. If you don't need the space and you are not up to it, allow them to stay. Bob's clothes stayed for at least a year. I had a son who I thought would want some of them, and in fact when he was large enough, he was very excited to wear his father's suits. (Of course, he didn't wear them very long since he rapidly grew past Bob's height). Remember, when you are ready to go through his personal items, your children may want some of them. They may want to have tangible memories of their father. It can be good to sort through things with adult children there to help.

Be aware that even after some time, when you go through his personal items, they will have an emotional effect. Bob always wore a particular brand of deodorant, but I despised the smell of that deodorant. In fact, I disliked it so much, he would go out of the room after he put it on. He usually put in on well in advance of my waking up so it would have a chance to air before I got up. Eight months after his death, I decided I really needed to clean off his side of the bathroom counter, rather than looking at his shaving gear, toothbrush, and deodorant everyday.

As I began sorting through Bob's toiletries, I discovered five containers of deodorant. Guessing that some of them were new and some of them were empty (he wasn't very good at throwing things away), I decided to open them. If they were new, I reasoned, my son, who was beginning to need deodorant, could use them. (I may not like the smell, but I am thrifty.) When I opened the first one I got an overwhelming whiff of this deodorant smell that I disliked so much. The next thing I knew, there I sat, crumpled on the bathroom floor, hugging an open can of deodorant and sobbing. I am sure it made quite a picture.

Unexpected things will trigger memories. Don't be shocked when it happens, just learn to accept these events as a normal part of the grieving process. Smell, sight, and sounds can all trigger tears. Even telling the story can make you cry again.

A friend, who was widowed four years before I was, explained this phenomenon to me a month after Bob died. She told of finding her husband's comb in the back of a bathroom drawer she was cleaning out, several years after her husband's death. Despite the fact that she had remarried, the comb reduced her to tears. As she told the story, her eyes became misty. Even retelling the event brought tears.

So, even when the time comes that you are comfortable with the idea of sorting out his stuff, be prepared for emotional reactions. If some things are too difficult to part with, pack them in a box and decide later. After my mother's death, I packed several boxes of things I couldn't part with. Many years later, a box filled with personalized notepaper surfaced. As I looked at it, I wondered what I planned to do with the paper. Time often clears up the conflict about what to keep and what to discard.

BE CAREFUL ABOUT UNSOLICITED FINANCIAL ADVICE

If you know how you want to handle investments and other financial matters, and you're good at it, do it. If you are unsure, seek out a qualified professional. If you have a family CPA or financial planner, they are a good place to start, but don't necessarily assume they are the right people to help you. Professionals, who also deal with other family members, may hear different goals and facts from different family members. Sometimes it is best to find someone who is working only for you.

The first step is to talk with the benefit planners from your husband's employer, if there are employment benefits. This person should be able to help you determine what financial benefits are available for you. Competent, trained assistance to help you budget, to determine what you can afford, and to set up an integrated financial plan covering both current expenses and your future security is essential.

Well-meaning family members, unless they have the qualifications and you trust them, are not the best choice. Family members who have not been successful in managing their own money should never be allowed to provide financial advice or assistance. Consider the possibility that, if you are getting a large sum of life insurance, you may not want family members to know. Often, what seems like a huge amount of money to somebody else is not a large amount when it must support you for the rest of your life. Opening your finances up to family members can result in requests to borrow money from you. Family members may view you as wealthy, and be hurt when you refuse to "lend" them money. It is hard to refuse to help your child or grandchild who has financial troubles, but at times it is necessary to protect your own future. Often, it is simply better not to discuss your finances with anyone except your financial planner, and to avoid the problem entirely.

The need for <u>competent</u> financial advice may be even greater if things are going to be tight financially. You may need professional advice to determine what you can and can't do. A competent financial planner can help you determine what assets must be sold and what funds you have available for providing for your living expenses and other needs. Family members mean well, but remember the old adage, you get what you pay for. If you are getting free advice, it may be worth just what you are paying for it.

When choosing a financial planner, check out his or her background and credentials. Before hiring anyone, consider the following:

- How long has he/she been active as a financial planner?
- Is the planner independent or employed by a specific company?
- Do you pay for his/her advice or do they receive a commission off the investments they sell you? (Commission is an incentive to sell you investments that pay the highest commission.)
- Does he/she have financial education beyond that provided by their company?

DON'T LISTEN TO FRIENDS' ADVICE ABOUT PROBATE

Clients frequently approach me with stories they have heard about the probate process. They are sure these things are true because it happened to "Aunt Bertha's husband's niece's hairdresser's mother." Some of the ones I hear most often include:

"I don't need to probate because everything goes to the spouse automatically." This is not true in Texas. Your husband's property does not transfer automatically, and who inherits is determined by his will. If he had no will, then state law determines who inherits. In either case, some probate process may be necessary.

"I don't need to probate, because my estate is under $100,000." Really, I don't have any idea where this comes from.

"If I don't have a will, the state gets everything." Not in Texas it doesn't. Your attorney can tell you who inherits without a will.

"The lawyer will take half of the estate." While I can't speak for all other attorneys, in my practice I bill on an hourly rate and most attorneys I know do the same. I know that some states mandate a percentage of the estate for attorney fees. Texas does not. With a properly drafted will, the probate should not cost that much.

"If I don't probate I won't have to pay taxes." If you owe them, you have to pay them. Period.

Depending on where you live, probate may be a problem. It may not. Do not take the advice of friends and do things without consulting a competent probate attorney.

A competent probate attorney should be able to tell you whether you need to probate, or whether there is a legal way to avoid the process. It is essential that you determine quickly if probate is required, what needs to be done, and the probable outcome. This is one step that should not be postponed. The attorney will ask a lot of questions, look at your husband's will or any trust he set up, and determine what is the best way to proceed.

In my probate practice, I frequently see women who have been told, by well- meaning friends, that they do not need to probate their husbands' wills because everything in Texas is community property. It is a common misconception that the community property passes automatically to the spouse on the death of the first spouse. This is absolutely not true. Sadly, I usually see them when they are trying to sell their house or get a home equity loan to make repairs and they suddenly discover they can do neither, because they do not own the house.

Under Texas probate, you only have four years in which to file a will. If you fail to file the will for probate within four years of death, you are unable to probate it. (There is a very narrow exception to that rule.) In many instances this makes no difference, as the wife may very well be her husband's legal heir. However, where there are blended families, failure to probate a will can result in your stepchildren owning their father's half of the estate, including the house. This can lead to some very difficult situations.

The best course is not to make assumptions. Don't act on the advice of friends. Get advice on legal matters from a <u>competent</u> probate attorney.

<u>THINK BEFORE YOU MOVE SOMEONE IN</u>

It wasn't long after my husband died that people decided my son and I shouldn't live alone, and that I needed someone to live with me and help me. Twice, over the course of several years, people moved in with me to "help" me. While I appreciated the willingness of family members to provide assistance, I quickly discovered that I was much more comfortable with just the two of us in my house. Over the years, several other people have offered to rent space from me, but, fortunately, by that time I was able to say no.

You must be careful in allowing people to come in to help. If you decide to allow a person to move in with you, make sure the ground rules are clear. If she is coming to help you, is she paying you rent? Are you getting services in lieu of rent, such as housekeeping, babysitting, driving children, or preparing meals? If they have kitchen privileges, are they required to clean up after themselves and in what time frame? Clarifying bathroom schedules, privacy issues, use of the garage, and so on, is necessary to make new living arrangements work.

Sometimes bringing someone in to help you can be a true gift, but sometimes the roommate becomes nothing but another child you need to take care of. At other times, a roommate may become demanding, overbearing, or even abusive. Make it very clear what you expect from the person, and that you have the right to ask her to leave at any time, if you are not comfortable continuing the relationship.

Be extremely cautious about allowing strangers to move in with you. If you need to take in a roommate for financial reasons, carefully check her background and references. I frequently hear stories of roommates, or live-in "boyfriends," who destroy houses, isolate and terrify the widow, and sometimes steal the unsuspecting widow's life savings. The problems roommates create may more than offset any money they paid you.

Before entering into any rental arrangement, check with a real estate attorney. Have the attorney draw a lease for you and determine what your rights are, and what rights the tenant has. Remember, if you have a paying tenant you want to leave, you may have to go to court to evict the roommate. Thorough preparation can avoid a lot of problems down the line. This will be more thoroughly covered in Chapter 3.

SLEEPING PILLS, ANTIDEPRESSANTS, OR TIME - YOU DECIDE

Depression can occur after the death of a spouse. Insomnia is even more frequent because you may be sleeping alone for the first time in many years. For most people these situations are transient and go away without treatment. Just because you are not as happy as other people want you to be, doesn't mean there is anything wrong with you. Remember, everybody grieves at their own pace.

Following my husband's death, I was very sad. Several months later a coworker told me she wanted the old Janet back – I was just too sad. She certainly couldn't have wanted the "old Janet" back any more than I did, but that Janet was gone forever. After the death of a spouse, you are never the same as you were before. Your situation has changed and it has fundamentally changed you. Can you become happy again? Of course you can, but you won't be the same. In time I became happy again, but it was a long process, and I will never again be the person I was before Bob's death.

21

If you believe you are really depressed, or you are troubled with continuing insomnia, and you feel it has gone on too long, consult your doctor. Properly used medication can help you through the roughest parts of your grief. You need sleep to be able to function and make good decisions. There are many safe drugs that can assist you in the process. Any intervention should be because you believe you need the assistance, not because your friends or family want "the old you" back. If you need help consult your doctor. DO NOT USE OTHER PEOPLE'S DRUGS or try to self-medicate. Only you and your doctor can decide if medical intervention is appropriate and would be beneficial for you. The use of sleeping pills or mood-altering drugs should only be under the supervision of your doctor.

DATING ON YOUR OWN TERMS

After a year or so, possibly less if you are younger, people will begin to decide you need to remarry. One friend of mine offered to set me up, telling me that women ruined their sons and I needed a man to help me raise my son. I, however, was not convinced that just anyone in trousers would be a suitable father for my child. Thomas needed my full attention, so I chose not to date. I have consistently refused friends' attempts to pair me up.

If you choose to date, be sure to do it on your own terms. Do not allow friends to push you into a premature relationship, and do not allow them to make decisions for you in terms of whom you date, how you date, and what that relationship will be. As with many aspects of the rebuilding of your life after your husband's death, dating and marriage have NO deadline.

In establishing a new relationship, especially after a long successful marriage, be aware of your children's feelings, especially young children. Do not be surprised if they are angry or resentful of the new relationship. Also, be cautious about introducing a new man into the household too early. Small children do not need to attach to a new man who may not be a permanent part of their lives. They have already suffered the loss of their father. They do not need another loss.

IT'S NOT HELP IF IT'S NOT WHAT YOU NEED

You have to look carefully at all well-meaning attempts to "help you." Most family members and friends simply want to see you happy. They want to make things better, but their understanding of your needs is driven by their perspective. Certainly listening to their advice may be beneficial, since alternate points of view are good to hear, in the end all of the decisions rest solely with you.

If you have been in a relationship where your spouse made most of the decisions, this may be a new, difficult experience. If that is the case, you may need to postpone some of the decision making until you are more confident about the decision. Major decisions should not be made in haste. You need to get competent professional help to help you explore the options and understand the impact of the decisions you are making. You must gather all the relevant facts and information before you can make a good decision.

You need to know that you can make the decisions that are required. You can stand on your own two feet, and take care of business. It requires patience with yourself, and with others. It requires that you seek out the information you need in order to make informed decisions. Most of all, it requires the tenacity to tell other people that you appreciate their input, but you will do what you believe is best for you and your family.

The following is a method I find helpful in making difficult decisions, especially in a crisis:

1. Define clearly what you are trying to decide. Without understanding the question you are asking, you cannot determine the best solution to the problem.

2. Find all the relevant facts. No competent decision can be made without adequate information.

3. List alternative courses of action. If you want to relocate, that could include such things as buying a new house, moving in with relatives, or moving to a retirement community.

4. List the pros (good effects) and cons (bad effects) of each choice. These can be based on your wants, emotional reactions, or practical aspects you may have discovered in your fact-finding.

5. List all your possible results and why you will choose or not choose them.

In the past, I have tried to do this process in my head. It is not nearly as effective as writing it down. I urge you to work through this in writing. An example of how to use this system and a blank form can be found in Appendix A. Write down <u>all</u> your thoughts. Remember, this is for you only - not for others to read. So write down everything that concerns you, no matter how silly it may seem. Using this will help you make sound decisions.

CHAPTER III

Living Alone or Living With Relatives

Independence vs. Dependence

Make decisions regarding your living arrangement, after carefully studying the relevant facts, based on what is best for YOU, not what your family and friends think.

My first piece of advice in the last chapter was never make a life-altering decision while you are in the early stages of grief, or preferably for at least a year. Changing your residence is one of those life-altering decisions. The decision to change your residence or your living arrangement cannot be made suddenly or without serious consideration. People often want to help, either by having you leave your home and move in with them, or by having someone move in with you. Both of those scenarios must be assessed in light of a number of conditions.

<u>MY STORY</u>

After Bob's death everyone assumed I would sell my house and move to a smaller one. Friends warned me that I couldn't possibly take care of the house by myself, that I couldn't afford the house, and that I would be afraid to live out in the country alone.

Family and friends tried to move in with me within days after the death. I was overwhelmed with well-meaning advice.

Following the advice I give to all new widows, I waited a year before making my decision. I chose to stay. Now my house is paid off and I love the seclusion of the country.

I also discovered that I preferred giving this advice to following it!

SELLING YOUR HOME AND MOVING IN WITH RELATIVES

If you are considering selling your home and moving in with relatives, there are some significant factors to consider. Each of these factors should be addressed when using the decision-making tool provided in the last chapter.

FINANCIAL

Two to three months after the death, you need to carefully and thoroughly assess your financial situation. To do this you must look at your income, and make a complete and thorough list of your assets and debts.

Next, make a list of your monthly expenses. Go back through the past year, using your checkbook, bank statements and credit card statements, and list expenses that occur monthly, quarterly, bi-annually, or annually. Those expenses that occur less than monthly need to be converted to a monthly figure. Add up quarterly or biannual ones to get your annual total, divide the annual total by twelve (12), and place the total in your monthly expenses. You need to include a monthly amount to cover occasional or emergency expenses. Be sure to include your monthly credit card purchases. They are part of your monthly expenses. (An example of a financial assessment form can be found in Appendix B.)

Compare your monthly expenses and income. Your monthly expenses should not be greater than your income. If your expenses are greater than your monthly earned or retirement income then you need to look at which expenses you can reduce or eliminate. Next, you need to look at your assets to determine if the income produced by your assets will be enough to cover your remaining expenses. When evaluating this, you also need to consider potential changes in your income and expenses. If you anticipate having your house paid off in two years, determine if you can continue to pay the mortgage for two years and how that will affect your expenses once it is paid off. Decide if paying the mortgage is going to deplete your savings too dramatically. If you have a child close to college age, you need to rapidly assess what you anticipate in terms of college costs. If you are close to retirement, adjust your income and expenses to what they will be when you retire to determine if your retirement income will be sufficient to support you.

Once you've determined what your expenses and income are, then you need to look at your current housing costs and compare it to the cost of living with somebody else. If you are considering moving in with a family member, you need to determine what rent or contribution to the household is expected. Is it a significant savings compared to what you're spending now? You must also consider the interest income on the money you will receive if you sell the house, after deducting the cost of any repairs you have to make to sell it, and the closing and real estate commission. Compare the cost of living with a relative to the cost of maintaining your own home. If moving in with a relative does not result in significant savings, then it may not be the best financial choice for you.

HEALTH CONCERNS

Once you've done all the financial work, you must honestly assess your ability to continue to live alone. If you are in good health, with no ongoing risk factors, staying at home alone may be acceptable. However, if you are at risk for sudden onset illness, i.e. heart attacks, uncontrolled diabetes, beginning Alzheimer's, frequent falls, or other diseases that require someone else to monitor you, then living alone in your own home may not be possible. If you have an adult child still living with you, staying at home may be reasonable, even with a debilitating illness. If you are unsure whether you need to have someone with you at all times, consult with your physician about what is needed to ensure your safety and health.

You also need to determine if you have the physical capability to keep the house in safe and sanitary condition, or if you are unable to, if you have the financial ability to hire someone to provide needed assistance. Do you have the physical ability to prepare meals? It is not healthy to eat a diet limited to canned food or dry cereal. If you are no longer able to cook reasonably healthy meals for one person, then you must either make arrangements for those meals to be eaten out or brought in, or you need to consider an alternative living arrangement.

Are you mentally alert enough and physically healthy enough to supervise your own medications? If you are on medications, you have to determine if you can sort those medications and be sure to take them in a timely fashion. Can you read the labels and open the bottles? (If there are no children in the home, you can ask for non-childproof caps.) If you are unsure if you can manage alone, work with a relative, friend or your doctor to determine if there is a way for you to manage your medications alone. If not, can it be done with occasional intervention, or do you need supervision all the time? Having someone help you set up a dose box once a week may be the only help you need. Before making any decision that affects your health, discuss all your options with your doctor.

EMOTIONAL STRESS

In addition to the financial and health concerns associated with selling your house, you have to look at the emotional impact of a sale and move. First, there is the impact of moving away from your memories. For some people, immediately after the death, there is the urge to run, to dispose of everything and escape from the painful memories. Unfortunately, the memories are inside you and you cannot run away from them.

A client of mine found the memories following her husband's death too hard to bear. Convinced she would be happy if she wasn't surrounded by people and things that were a constant reminder of her loss, she sold her house, disposed of his possessions, and moved away to get a "fresh start." Two years later, she moved back. The excitement of being on her own, and doing something new, had lasted about six months. Then she began sinking into loneliness and depression. She moved back to be near people who cared about her.

For some, the thought of disposing of anything and leaving the family home is unbearable. Each item holds a memory too precious to lose. The attachment to things is understandable. They are physical links to the past that you can hold and touch. Be careful that it doesn't become an unhealthy desire to continue living in the past, rather than moving forward and establishing your new life. Your house should be your home, not a shrine to your deceased husband. The emotional effect of leaving the house, or staying, has to be weighed against the financial and physical factors discussed above.

There are people who are absolutely terrified of living alone. The fear of being trapped and isolated in the house or of having no one with whom to have a conversation can be overwhelming. For a person who needs constant social interaction, living alone may not be a good choice.

If your choice is to sell your house and move in with one of your children, you need to determine how much time the family will be spending at home to provide company. Moving into your child's house and staying by yourself ten or eleven hours a day, while family members are at work or engaged in their own social lives, may be no more comfort than living alone. If there are small children in the household, you may become a built-in babysitter or find yourself left alone in the evenings, while family members attend child-related events. If you need companionship, this may not provide it.

Think carefully about the emotional effects of living alone before you make the choice to move. As an alternative to moving for companionship, consider finding activities outside your home to provide social interaction. Does a church near you have a seniors' group or a mission project that might interest you? Check for activities in your community at the community center, the library, the senior center, and the local food pantry. But don't limit yourself. Consider taking the literature course, cake decorating class, or sculpting class you always wanted to take. Check with the local colleges for continuing education classes.

Or, if you are more ambitious, sign up for college courses and get that degree you always wanted. Begin the career you dreamed of, but gave up to have a family. Part time work or volunteer work will keep your mind occupied. Norman Vincent Peal in The Power of Positive Thinking tells stories of people who conquered grief by finding a meaningful and fulfilling activity. He asserts that those grieving must avoid the temptation to sit and brood. It is good advice.

ASSESS YOUR ABILITY TO GET AROUND

Before deciding whether to sell your house and move in with someone else, you must determine how you will get around. Some women have become used to having a spouse to take them everywhere. Recent widows, older women in particular, find themselves uncomfortable driving places and traveling alone, even to such familiar places as church. If you don't have the ability to take yourself to the grocery store, to church, to the doctor, and to other necessary locations, living alone may result in a sense of social isolation.

If you are able to drive, if you work, if you have plenty of social interaction outside of the home, coming home to an empty house may not pose an issue for you. It may, instead, be a place where you can rest and recover.

SECURITY CONCERNS

If living alone frightens you, consider getting a security system. Talk with family and friends about who they use to provide home security. Have someone you trust, who is knowledgeable about security systems, with you when you meet with security sales people. DO NOT sign up for a system you do not understand, or are not sure you can operate. ALWAYS have any service contract you are going to sign reviewed by your attorney BEFORE you sign it. Legitimate companies will still be there after you meet with your attorney and if they object to you taking the time to review the contract, move on to another company.

Another option is a dog. While most dogs kept as pets are not trained for security, many can be trained to alert you when there is someone outside. Of course, a hypersensitive dog may alert you to every raccoon, squirrel, cat, and gust of wind that passes through the neighborhood. Dogs require walking, feeding, vet visits, scooping the yard, and a lot of affection, so be sure you can provide those things before you get a dog.

While having someone in the house may provide a sense of security, it may be time to fearlessly confront the reality of living alone. Ask yourself how many times your husband actually confronted an intruder in your home. If the answer is several, then it may be time to consider the safety of the neighborhood in which you live. If the answer was never, then remind yourself that the fear may not be based in fact.

If your answer is, as mine was, never, then consider the odds of something occurring based on past experience. That should give you a lot of confidence in staying at home. Focusing on meditation, prayer, or relaxation exercises can help you in getting to sleep. Also, the short-term use of sleeping medication or anti-anxiety medication, prescribed by your doctor, may be beneficial in helping you adjust to nights spent alone. The transition does not take as long as you might think. After several months, I was able to sleep through the night.

MINOR CHILDREN

If you are a young widow with minor children, you need to ask yourself if you can manage the children, the house, and a job alone. No matter how competent you are, it is not always possible to do everything yourself. You will need to find competent, trustworthy, repair services for plumbing, electrical, appliances, and other things that may break. If you do not believe you can manage alone, then moving in with a relative may be beneficial. Before moving, you should consider your financial situation, as discussed above. You should also consider the children's ages and the school district they are in versus the district they will be in if you move. Fearlessly assess the amount of time you will have to give to your job to generate enough income to cover all the family expenses. The cost of childcare while you are at work should be considered in any decision to move.

The emotional impact on the children should be considered. If your child is a high school senior or preparing to do an Eagle Scout project with the boys he has known since 1st grade, then you may want to delay a move until high school graduation, the Eagle Scout ceremony, or other important events have occurred.

SUPPORT OF FRIENDS

The last thing you need to consider is the ability to develop new friendships where you move. The loss of all of your close and supportive friends, including those who may be able to help you get children to and from activities, may result in a type of social isolation. Be sure, before you move, that the move is in your and your children's best interest.

HAVING SOMEONE MOVE IN WITH YOU

An option, that allows you to stay in your own home, is having someone move in with you. Before allowing someone to move in with you, you need to make many of the same assessments described above, but there are several additional things to consider.

Will The Person Be A Paid Renter, A Helper, Or Just A Companion?

As I mentioned in Chapter 2, the ground rules of why a person is living with you must be clear. How much rent will she pay? If the goal is to provide you with some financial assistance, she needs to understand that the rent must be paid in a timely fashion, and that you cannot financially support her. This must be very clear with regard to family members who may decide that it is okay not to pay you when finances get tight.

If the person is moving in to "help" you, the terms of that help must be clear and precise before they move in. It is not helpful to have someone move in with you who is going to cook in your kitchen, only to come home from work and find a huge mess that you must clean up before you can make your own dinner. If you have small children, and the person is coming to "help" you with your children, you need to make it clear what that encompasses. Do you need her (or him) to be there every Thursday night while you have a late meeting at the office? Do you expect her to watch your child while you're out of town? Do you need her to drive the child to and from evening activities? Make it crystal clear what is expected before the person moves in with you. The terms of your agreement should be in writing. Before allowing anyone to move into your house, consult a licensed real estate attorney and have him/her draw up the lease for you.

If the person is there simply to provide companionship, ground rules need to be set to make sure you each have your own personal space, private family time, rules concerning TV sharing, kitchen privileges, having guests of the opposite sex, and any other issues of concern. Rules regarding hours of coming and going, noise levels, and housekeeping, need to be set out in writing with the other expectations. All of the ground rules for someone moving in with you must be clear, based on what their role is to be in the household. Two specific issues that should be clearly addressed are smoking in the house and pets. As with any rental agreement, your ability to ask them to leave must be spelled out. **Do Not** draft any lease by yourself. Consult your attorney.

CONSIDER COMPATIBLE LIFESTYLES

Before allowing someone to move in with you, determine what type of lifestyle that person lives. If you tend to go to bed at eight o'clock at night, you may not want a "twenty-something" playing rock music at midnight in the bedroom next to you. If you do not get up until eight or eight-thirty in the morning, you may not want to hear the shower going at four in the morning while you want to sleep. You need to confirm who is going to be cooking, cleaning, and, if you are to be sharing food, who is buying, and what the obligations are. If you are sharing food and cooking chores, you need to know if there are food issues that will have to be addressed, such as food allergies and preferences. Beware of conflicts that can occur when you are constantly buying groceries that simply get eaten because they're in the refrigerator. This is most likely to occur with someone who has been living with his or her parents, was supported by them, and is used to unlimited access to the household foods.

ASSESS YOUR ATTITUDE TOWARD INVASION OF YOUR SPACE

In the time immediately following the death, you often need to have people around you, but at the same time, having somebody who does not do things the way you're used to can create frustration and anger. Before embarking on a house-sharing arrangement, you need to look closely at yourself and determine if you are willing to accept changes in the household, and changes in the way things are done. Somebody who comes in to help will want to do things his or her way, and that may not be your way. If you are unsure about compatibility between you and your proposed housemate, or if you are unsure about your ability to accommodate anyone else's needs during your time of grief and recovery, then delay having someone live with you while you more thoroughly assess your state of mind.

Finally, recognize that you are hurting, that your life has been disrupted, and that unless there is a financial crisis, the decisions <u>do not</u> have to be made today. If relatives are clamoring to move in with you, simply tell them you have not decided. Do not allow yourself to be pushed into doing something you are not sure you are ready for. Once they've moved in, it will be very hard to ask them to leave. Even after a trial period, it is nearly impossible to get people to leave without damaging the relationship, so be cautious in allowing them to come stay with you for "a few days." A few days can turn into a lifetime.

Before embarking on a house-sharing arrangement, whether it involves rent or not, it is essential to have an agreement drawn up by your attorney. It should include all the issues touched on in this chapter, and any other issues you feel are important, and the relevant legal issues such as breach of contract, eviction, and damages. Such an agreement is necessary to give you the tools to force housemates to move out, should they breach the agreement.

While you may think a written agreement is not necessary, I would strongly urge you to consult with a Probate or Real Estate attorney to help you determine how best to ensure that any transaction you enter into will be in your best interest.

CHAPTER IV

Dollars and Sense

Full Financial Checkup

> Assess your financial condition honestly and then
>
> sit down with your CPA or other advisor and set up a
> plan for managing your assets and paying your bills.

Financial decisions are very important to a new widow. Often the new widow is faced with dramatically reduced income, while the expenses stay the same. A full financial checkup should be done in the weeks following the death.

MY STORY

Immediately after my husband died, between his death and the funeral, as I struggled to recover from the initial shock, the next shockwave rolled over me. I realized that, despite my employment as an attorney, I had just lost the primary breadwinner for the family. My husband had provided the bulk of our income, since my practice, while busy, was small at that time. Additionally, all of the insurance and benefits ran through my husband's employer.

As panic set in, I pulled out our estimate of benefits for the year and discovered, to my horror, that my situation was worse than I had realized. The annuity I received would be small. In addition, it would be reduced by one half the Social Security benefits I would be entitled to receive, whether I actually received them or not.

The second major shock was that our pension election, to have my husband receive a smaller monthly pension and for me to receive half of it at his death, only applied if Bob were already retired when he died. Since he died during active service, I would receive a one-time payment equal to his annual salary, and no retirement benefit. I was stunned!

My husband had failed to take out the maximum amount of life insurance available, although he intended to. Instead, he had the same amount of insurance he took out in 1980, when we got married, had no children, and our mortgage payment was $120.00 a month. The amount of the insurance was enough to pay for the funeral and part of my husband's credit card debts.

As I ran through my options, I felt a pervasive sense of despair. The news was nearly as devastating as his death. The only upside in this was my husband had been employed long enough so that we got to keep our health insurance.

GATHERING ASSET INFORMATION

One of the first things you are going to have to do after your husband's death is a full financial checkup. To begin, you need to make a list of all of the assets you have.

1. <u>Start with your home.</u> Determine how much it's worth, and how much is still owed on the mortgage. A property tax statement can give you an idea of the value (though it may not be accurate in this volatile economy), and a mortgage statement can tell you what is owed.

2. <u>Find copies of the most recent bank statements</u> for all checking, savings, CDs, and other bank accounts for you or your spouse, and determine how much is in each account. You also need to determine if that account is a joint account with the Right of Survivorship with you or some other person. If it is Right of Survivorship with you, it should belong to you. If it goes to some other person, then you need to separate it from yours, because it will not be available for you.

Joint accounts that are not Right of Survivorship and assets in your husband's name will all need to pass through the probate process, and your husband's will or a Court will determine to whom his portion belongs.

3. <u>Find statements for all stock accounts</u> and brokerage accounts belonging to you or your husband. Once again, determine whose name they are in, the value of the account, if they are Right of Survivorship, or if

there is a beneficiary on the account. In other words, does it go to a specific person upon death? If that person is not you, then separate it from yours.

4. List all of the individual retirement accounts that you and your husband have, whom the beneficiaries are on the accounts, and the value of them. If someone other than you is the beneficiary of your husband's IRA, separate it from yours.

5. Look for 401Ks, retirement plans, thrift savings accounts, and other things through an employer. Identify any beneficiary on those and list their value.

6. Locate life insurance policies. Determine if there is privately held life insurance or life insurance through an employer. List all of those policies, the death value, and who the beneficiaries are.

7. List any other thing of value, including club memberships, major jewelry, ownership in businesses, partnerships, business equipment, cars, planes, major tools and yard equipment. All of those things need to be listed individually, with their value noted.

You will need this information for your assessment of your financial situation. You will also provide copies of these documents to your probate attorney. She will help you determine what belongs in your husband's estate.

Assets to search for:

- House

- Vacation home
- Timeshares
- Lake lots
- Inherited real estate
- Mineral rights
- Cars/Trucks
- Airplanes
- Collectibles
- Artwork
- Bank accounts
- CD's
- Stocks/Brokerage accounts
- IRA
- 401Ks
- College savings accounts
- Credit unions
- Savings bonds
- Employee thrift/Saving plans
- Jointly owned property
- Businesses/Partnerships
- Assets in safety deposit box
- Cash
- Life insurance
- Notes/Mortgages payable to you

INCOME

To determine what your income is going to be, list all sources of income that will continue.

1. List <u>your</u> earned income, if you have any. List both your gross pay and your take-home pay, after all deductions.

2. List <u>your</u> retirement income. List the gross amount you receive and the net amount, the net being what you actually receive after all deductions.

3. If you currently receive Social Security income, VA pension, or other forms of government retirement income, list the total amount and the net amount you receive after all deductions.

4. Having listed all of your income, it is now necessary to list all income you will receive as a result of your spouse's death. If your spouse was still employed, look to see if there is salary continuation insurance or annuity that will begin upon his death. The personnel or benefits department of his employer should know that answer. If there is, determine approximately what it will be, when you will receive it, and for how long. List the gross and the net.

If you are retirement age and will receive a portion of his retirement, list the portion that you will receive. Be sure and discuss with his employer any offsets against the monthly payment. If you and your husband were both drawing Social Security, you may be able to draw a portion of his Social Security plus your Social Security. If your Social Security is greater or equal to your husband's, you will not receive an increase.

List the income from bank accounts and stock accounts that belong to you outright (not those that go to other persons, or which must be handled through the Probate Court).

Income Sources:

- Employment (yours)
- Employment annuity (his)
- Retirement (yours)
- Retirement benefit (his)
- Social Security
- Annuity
- Income from business or partnership
- Interest - Bank accounts
- Dividends/Stock
- Rent
- Payment of loans/Mortgages you hold

DEBTS

Next, list your debts. Start with those secured by liens and then unsecured debt. List your home mortgage. List the total amount that is still owed (most likely you can find this on your statement), and the amount of the payment. Do the same for any other real estate you have. If you have car notes, identify the car, how much is still due on the note, and your payment. For credit cards and loans, identify each credit card separately, each loan separately, or any other obligation you have separately. Identify the total amount you owe and the total amount of the monthly payment.

LIVING EXPENSES

Go through three (3) months worth of bank statements, your check book, and credit card statements, and determine how much it will take to continue to live. You should list all of your expenses, starting with mortgage, car payment, taxes, insurance, utility payments, and working down through credit card payments, food, and gas. Do this for a minimum of three (3) months, listing expenses by month, so that you can identify approximately how much it is going to cost you to live. An example of an Expense Worksheet is included in Appendix B.

DETERMINING YOUR NET WORTH

Next, you are going to make a net worth statement. On the left hand side of the page you will list all of your assets. On the right hand side, you will list all of your debts (liabilities).

Once you have gathered the information and determined what is available to live on, you can begin making plans. A competent financial planner can help you decide how to invest your assets to produce the best results based on your financial needs and goals.

Add up the total for each column. Take the total value of the assets and subtract the total value of the debts from it. That will tell you how much your estate is worth.

After that, do the same for your income and expenses. List all your sources of income on one side, and all of your expenses on the other side. Add up the total for each column. Subtract your total expenses from your total monthly income and that will tell you how much extra you will have each month, or how much you will need to supplement your income from your assets to pay monthly expenses.

Forms for a net worth statement can be found in Appendix C. However, the use of a computer financial program will allow you, not only to figure net worth and income/expenses, but to track and manage your assets in the future.

DEALING WITH THE ESTATE

Once you have done this financial checkup, you need to determine what, if any, of your jointly held assets you will inherit. It will be necessary for you to have an attorney review the will and determine if you or somebody else will inherit his assets. If there is no will, it is imperative that you go immediately to a competent probate attorney and determine who will inherit under the state law. In Texas, if your spouse had children from outside your marriage, they may inherit his half of your community property (including the homestead) and a portion of his separate property. It is essential, when doing your financial checkup, to determine which of the assets will belong to you so that you can accurately determine what you have available to live on.

INSURANCE

If you are not yet qualified for Medicare, you must determine if you will be able to keep your health insurance if it is provided through your husband's job. If you have insurance from your employer, then this is not critical. If you were dependent on his job for insurance, it is important that you determine quickly what health insurance benefits will continue, for how long, and what the cost will be. If you will not be allowed to continue group insurance, you may be allowed to continue it for up to eighteen months under <u>COBRA</u>, but you will have to pay privately for it. This will give you an opportunity to purchase private health insurance or move into a job that provides health insurance benefits. Without health insurance benefits, your financial situation is precarious.

If you have no insurance, it is important that you buy at least a catastrophic policy to cover you until you can get insurance through an employer. If you have minor children, you may be able to insure them through a state program for uninsured children. Check on the internet or with the state or local health department to find a program.

Remember, if you are having to pay personally for health insurance be sure that figure is in your expense calculations.

Once you have all your assets, debt, and legal information together, it is a good time to sit down with your CPA or other advisor and set up a plan for managing your assets and paying your bills. Be prepared to seek new employment, cut expenses, or make other changes required by your new financial situation.

CHAPTER V

Keep It Legal

The first thing you need to do to begin the
legal process is to find a competent, qualified,
probate attorney.

The legal aspects of dealing with the death of a
spouse are daunting and sometimes a little frightening.
Dealing with the legal issues soon after death as possible
will make the transition easier for you.

MY STORY

Shortly after my husband died, I was forced to
deal with the many legal issues that face a new widow. I
found, much to my surprise, that despite the fact I had
been a probate and an estate planning attorney for many
years, I was as shocked and scattered as all the widows I
dealt with. I much preferred giving advice to having to
follow that same advice. The very first thing I was forced
to do was look at the probate of my husband's estate. I
had walked into Probate Court many times with many
different people, yet when it came time to walk into that
Court to probate my husband's will, I found myself
pacing outside the door, reluctant to go in, to
acknowledge that Bob was dead, and finalize that chapter
of my life.

Shortly after the probate, a number of additional legal decisions had to be made. My will had to be redrawn. New executors and new guardians for my minor child were necessary. There were questions about who would handle money for him, who would take care of him - all those things that had only been a vague concern as long as I had my husband to take care of our son if I died. At a time when you are most vulnerable, when you hurt more than you thought was possible, when it is hard to make sound decisions, you, as a new widow, are faced with a long list of things that must be done in an orderly fashion, and in a fairly quick time frame.

FINDING AN ATTORNEY

The first thing you need to do to begin the legal process is to find a competent, qualified, probate attorney. I strongly suggest that you speak with friends who have gone through this process and have had experience with probate attorneys. Ask if they felt their attorney took care of their problems in a timely fashion and handled it professionally. Ask for referrals from several trusted sources. It is important that you find an attorney who is very familiar with the probate process, especially if your spouse died without a will. It is equally important that you find an attorney you are comfortable with.

Under Texas law, if a person dies without a will, the property **does not** automatically go to the spouse, as many people presume. It is sometimes necessary to have a Court determine who the person's heirs are, even when that seems clear to everyone involved. It may then be necessary for the Court to appoint a Court supervised

Administrator to handle the closing out of the deceased's affairs. If no will exists, it is extremely important that you have an experienced attorney to guide you through this process.

If you do not know a probate attorney, or if you cannot find one through a friend, try the local Bar Association. Ask about the attorney's credentials. Board Certification is an indication of education and experience, but it is not essential. You will want to ask how long he/she has handled probate, how many probates they handle a year, if he/she has ever done a probate without a will, and how often is he/she in Probate Court in your county. When you meet with the attorney, if you are uncomfortable, take some time to think about it before employing that attorney or signing a contract. If you are uncomfortable with the proposed charges, meet with another attorney before making a decision. You will be spending a considerable amount of time working with your attorney. It is important that you hire someone you trust, and with whom you can have a good working relationship.

PROBATING THE ESTATE

After the death of a person who owned property, a probate is usually required. If there is a will, the will is taken to the attorney, and the attorney files an Application with the Court. After a waiting period, the attorney and the client go to Court to prove up the facts surrounding the death and the validity of the will. Most of the time, when there is a valid Texas will, the hearing is brief. The Executor is appointed at the hearing and the

Court process is nearly complete. Where there is no will, an heirship proceeding may be needed, and it is more difficult and time consuming.

When you meet with your probate attorney for the first time, you should take the following things:

- The original will of your deceased spouse
- A copy of the will if you are not sure where the original is
- A copy of the death certificate, if you have it
- All the relevant information on the deceased person
  - Name,
  - Address
  - Date of birth
  - Date of death
  - County in which they lived
  - Names and ages of all their children
  - Names of anyone they have divorced from and the dates of all of their divorces
  - Parent's names and whether they are still living
- Addresses of all of the people who receive a gift in the will
- A detailed list of assets, and whether these assets belong to both spouses or belong only to the deceased spouse
- For each asset owned at the time of death bring a description and value

Being prepared, and bringing as much information as possible, will help keep your costs low. It is a good idea to bring copies of bank statements, stock statements, tax statements for real estate, car titles, and any other financial information that will help the attorney prepare the probate.

Probate of the will should be started as quickly as possible after the death. Under Texas law, the will cannot be probated if more than four (4) years have passed since the date of death. Additionally, the more time that passes, the more difficult it will be to deal with any problems with the will. Sometimes probate may require finding witnesses or people who recognize the deceased person's handwriting. The longer you wait, the harder it is to find people to testify.

Where there is no will, you should bring all of the information listed above, plus the names, addresses, and phone numbers of two people who know the deceased's family history personally, and who will not inherit from him. These two people should know him well enough to attest to his family history, marital history and children, and be willing to appear in Court to testify. They can be relatives who will not inherit or longtime friends.

STEPCHILDREN

A problem that often occurs following the death of a spouse is dealing with the stepchildren. Stepchildren, who have been easy to deal with during the marriage, may become difficult, and those who have been difficult to deal with often become impossible. They will demand what they believe is their share of the inheritance immediately. Under no circumstances should you give anyone unsupervised access to the house, especially if you believe they may remove anything, nor should you give away estate property without consulting an attorney. Do not allow anyone to remove important paperwork from the house, as this can result in the loss of financial information, tax information, and, worst of all, the original will. (The loss of an original will, in one case I handled, caused the estate to drag out for eight years. It was believed that a child of the deceased had removed the original will, along with other vital paperwork immediately after death, before the spouse even got home from the hospital.)

Stepchildren, ex-spouses, and other family members who believe they are entitled to a portion of the deceased's property, should be told firmly that nothing can be disposed of until after the probate has been completed. Should they insist, or should you become concerned about them removing things without your permission, contact your attorney, and with your attorney's consent, change the locks. Typically, this is a time when your resistance to pressure is low. Call on your attorney to assist you and to determine what your rights are.

INSURANCE

In the days following the funeral, you should begin gathering insurance policies and contacting each of the companies to ask for beneficiary information and appropriate forms for filing. Most insurance policies cannot be handled until you have a death certificate; however, they are often willing to send you the paperwork in advance. If the insurance is made payable to the estate, in most states you will not be able to cash it until the estate has been opened and an Executor appointed. If the insurance is payable to someone other than you, the insurance company usually will not forward you the paperwork, nor tell you who the beneficiary is. If you are the beneficiary of the insurance, the insurance company should forward you all of the paperwork, which you will return with the death certificate to collect the insurance. If you are unsure about how to fill out the paperwork, consult your attorney for instructions and review.

EMPLOYEE BENEFITS

As previously discussed in Chapter 4, you need to contact the company that your husband worked for as quickly as possible. Talk with the benefits' office to determine what the death benefits are, and if the benefits are assigned to you or to some other party. The company will need a copy of the death certificate when you get it, and should assist you in securing any benefits that are due to you. If you are uncertain about your husband's benefits, ask the benefit's specialist to check on insurance, annuities, retirement funds, 401k, thrift plan, any money remaining in flexible spending accounts and how long you have to spend it, and any optional insurance. Be sure and check on the status of health insurance, if you are insured through your husband's employer, to determine if the insurance will continue for you and your children. If not, ask if you may be able to apply for Cobra to continue (and pay for it) long enough to secure insurance on your own. Additional paperwork that may be needed includes your marriage license, birth certificates for you and your children, and Social Security numbers for everyone.

OTHER LEGAL STUFF

There are a number of other people you should notify of your husband's death:

1. The credit bureau. You should let the major credit bureaus know of the death of your husband. They will flag the account to prevent anyone from opening new accounts or reviving dormant accounts. This is necessary to protect your finances from identity theft.

2. Credit cards. Legally you cannot continue to use credit cards after the death of the owner of the card. You must contact the credit card companies and let them know that he is deceased. If the card is held by both of you and you want to continue to use it, take the necessary steps to get it transferred into your name. It is important, if your spouse had a card that was being used by somebody else, i.e., a child or other relative, that the use be stopped. The person holding the card should be notified immediately that you have contacted the credit card company and instructed them not to allow any more charges, since the card owner is deceased.

3. Social Security. In general, funeral homes contact Social Security. You will want to contact Social Security to discuss any benefits you may be entitled to or that your minor children may be entitled to. Also, if your spouse was drawing Social Security, be aware that the

Social Security payment for the month he died will be withdrawn from your bank account. If the withdrawal is going to cause an undue financial hardship, you need to get directions from Social Security on how to file a hardship request and ask them not to withdraw it.

NEW DOCUMENTS FOR YOU

After dealing with the immediate issues surrounding the death, you need to look at your own legal picture. This means sitting down with a competent estate planning attorney and reviewing a number of documents.

LAST WILL AND TESTAMENT

Your will should be reviewed and rewritten to reflect your new status. If you have minor children, you will need to appoint a guardian and an alternate, as well as a financial trustee and an alternate. If you had your spouse as your Executor, you need to appoint a new Executor, and an alternate. The disposition of your estate will need to be reviewed. Determine who you want to have your property at your death, and rewrite your will accordingly. Contrary to what you may have heard, in Texas there is no requirement that you leave $1.00 to anyone. You may leave your property to anyone, as long as you are competent to do so. Even if your will and your husband's will were made at the same time, with a common plan, there is no requirement that you keep that plan after his death.

Internet and "do-it-yourself" wills have become very popular in recent years. I would discourage you from using these services, as the wills drawn this way are often defective and sometimes not able to be probated. The small amount of money you save is often more than offset by the much more costly probate as a result.

POWER OF ATTORNEY

A Durable Power of Attorney appoints somebody to handle your finances for you if you cannot handle them yourself. This may not have seemed particularly important while you were married. It is of critical importance when you are no longer married. A <u>Durable</u> Power of Attorney is one that continues into your incapacity. It allows someone to deal with your bank accounts, pay your bills, manage your home, sell your car, or anything that needs to be done. In the absence of a Power of Attorney, should you become incapacitated, family members will be forced to get a legal guardianship over you. Guardianship in Texas requires Court supervision and permission from the Court for all expenditures. This is a lengthy and expensive process that you will want to avoid if you have a family member or friend you trust to handle your affairs.

MEDICAL POWER OF ATTORNEY

While your husband was alive, he was automatically allowed to make medical decisions for you. Now that you are unmarried, it is necessary for you to appoint someone to make medical decisions for you. You may have previously had a Medical Power of Attorney, with your spouse as your first choice, and a child as an alternate. Look closely at which person in your life will be most able to make hard decisions in a crisis. That person should be appointed to make your medical decisions. I encourage you not to appoint two children to be co-decision makers. While this seems like a good idea, the reality is that ,should they disagree, the doctors will not know who is entitled to make that decision, and it can dramatically impact the quality of your care. Select the person you believe will be best in that situation. Appoint that person as decision maker, and put the second best person in as the alternate. If you feel you must appoint co-decision makers, discuss the implications carefully with your attorney.

DIRECTIVE TO PHYSICIANS (LIVING WILL)

A Living Will is a very personal document. It expresses your wishes in the event that you are terminally ill or in a permanently incapacitated state. This document, without regard to your choices, will be a huge gift to your family when they have to make hard decisions for you at the end of your life. Any decision you make should be clearly explained to your medical decision maker in advance of a crisis. It is important to know that they will honor your wishes.

These are the basic documents you will need to ensure that your wishes are followed. A copy of a booklet, "Important Information For Your Family" is found in Appendix D. Copy it, fill in the information, and keep it with your documents. I encourage everyone to have these documents prepared as quickly as possible following the death of a spouse. Remember, these documents can be changed when your situation and needs change, as long as you are competent to do so. They probably will be changed as time goes by and the grief begins to lesson. You may decide the choices you made initially after the death do not match what you want at a later time. So make the best decisions you can, and be comfortable knowing that you have taken care of your legal needs.

CHAPTER VI

Home Sweet Home (or not!)

Before you make any decision about moving or staying, get solid advice from your attorney and from your accountant. Well-meaning advice from other people is just that - well meaning, but they are not living your life and do not know what your needs are.

To move or not to move, that is the question nearly every new widow faces. The decision can be extremely difficult, but you can make the choice that is right for you.

MY STORY

Within days after my husband's death, people began asking me when I was going to sell the house. The first person approached me with this question at the funeral! Friends who were real estate agents approached me. Friends who were not real estate agents approached me. Everyone assumed that because I lived in a fairly large house, I would immediately be dumping my house. Of course, people also asked me if they could buy my husband's truck, my husband's tools, and his lawn tractor. "Exactly how was I supposed to mow the lawn?" I wondered. The decision to stay in your home or move is a very personal one. I consistently told people that I would not be selling my home at that time. People continued to encourage me to sell my home, telling me I could not possibly manage the payments by myself, couldn't keep the house up, would be afraid in the country without my husband, etc. (I have now paid off my home and enjoy living in the relative seclusion of the countryside.)

DECIDING TO KEEP OR SELL YOUR HOME

CONSIDERATIONS WHEN SELLING YOUR HOME

Probate Considerations

In general, the house cannot be sold until after the probate is completed, so it may be several months before you can do anything with the house. It will be necessary to consult a probate attorney to determine where your husband's part of a jointly held property will go. In Texas, owning property in both names, even the community property homestead, does not mean it will go automatically to the surviving spouse. Where there is no will, in Texas, the property will pass based on a statutory formula.

Consulting your probate attorney is the first step in determining what you want to do. Do not make assumptions about what will happen to the property based on your friends' experience, advice from well-meaning relatives, or the internet. Get advice from an attorney who works regularly in probate.

Financial

The next thing you need to look at is your finances. If you can make the immediate payments on your mortgage, continue to do so. This gives you time to assess your finances before making a decision.

1. <u>Determine if you can make the payments out of your current income.</u> If you are unable to make the payments, and are in danger of defaulting on the loan, then it will become apparent fairly quickly that you must sell the house. If you can make the payments, I encourage you to wait a year before making a decision. If you absolutely cannot make the payments or you know you can only manage the payments for a few months, then it may be necessary to get the house on the market as quickly as you can after the probate process is complete.

2. <u>Assess your income potential.</u> Even if you don't have enough income from your current job, determine if you will be able to get a better paying job that will allow you to pay the mortgage. If not, will there be enough interest off investments to allow you to pay your note and live comfortably?

3. <u>Check your insurance.</u> Is there an insurance policy specifically to pay off the house on death? If you had insurance, then the house may be paid off for you. Check with your mortgage company to see if there was insurance. If there is, you need to contact them immediately and provide them with the necessary documentation.

4. <u>Locate your life insurance policies.</u> Is there sufficient life insurance available to pay off the house and meet your other needs? You must determine if the best use of any life insurance is to pay off the house. In making this assessment, you need to look at your income and all other sources of funds to determine if paying off the house will allow you to pay all of your monthly expenses with your current income. Be sure to consider insurance and taxes on the house, which may currently be paid in your mortgage payment, but will still be due even after the house is paid off. Prior to paying off the house, you need to determine what the annual taxes and insurance are, and if you can continue to pay those out of your monthly income, as well as all of your other monthly expenses.

To determine if you can afford the taxes and insurance on the house, take all of your monthly expenses and list them. Then take the total taxes for one year and the total insurance for one year, and divide those figures by twelve (12). Add $1/12^{th}$ of each figure to your list of monthly expenses. If you have other expenses paid annually, they should be figured the same way.

Add all of your monthly bills and expenses, including the monthly cost of annual items, together and determine if your income is enough to cover all of those expenses. Bear in mind as you add those expenses to include upkeep and repairs on the house, repairs on your cars, and all living expenses, such as food, clothes, gasoline, medical care, and other necessities. If you determine that you have sufficient income, you need to set up a separate bank account where you will deposit the money for the taxes and insurance each month, so that when the payments come due, you will have the full amount ready to pay.

5. It may be possible to pay off the house with existing savings. If you have enough savings and income to cover all your needs, plus enough to pay off the house, then your savings can be used to pay off the house. Before using savings or life insurance to pay off the house, determine whether this will benefit you. If you are early in your note, and paying mostly interest, then paying off the house may have tremendous savings for you over the long run. On the other hand, if you are two or three years away from paying off the house and you are paying mostly principle, there will not be a significant interest savings.

It is very important that you consult your CPA for assistance in determining all the tax and other implications of paying off your house. You should discuss your financial situation with your CPA prior to deciding to pay off your house.

Personal and emotional reasons involved in the decision to sell

There are a number of personal and emotional reasons that you have to consider before deciding to sell. For most people, there is an emotional attachment to the house. For some people, memories of living in the house as a couple make it difficult to move, and others feel the need to get away from the painful memories. Because of the emotional nature of this, I encourage you to take some time before making any decision. Once you have sold the house it is not possible to go back and rethink that choice, so it is important that you let your emotions settle before you decide.

A personal matter to be considered is your children. If you have children who are still in school, you may want to look at the effect that moving to a new school will have on the children. If you have a high school senior, you will probably not want to move until the child has completed his senior year in high school. With any high school age children, you may want to stay for their benefit. With younger children, the move may not be as traumatic in terms of school, but you will want to assess the quality of the school district you are currently in, as opposed to the school district you would be moving to.

Another consideration in the decision to move is the loss of friends and support system. If you move into a new community, you will often lose the support of your neighbors, church, and other friends. That loss of support can leave you feeling isolated and alone, and can be very detrimental to your emotional well-being, especially during the first year. However, moving closer to family can be very helpful. Determine if the move will be beneficial emotionally. If you believe it will not be emotionally beneficial, but it is financially necessary to make the move, then you need to find a way to maintain a connection with people who will provide you with the necessary emotional support.

Practical Considerations

Where are you going to move? It is easy to say, "I'm going to sell the house and move." Before you do so, you have to determine where you are going to move and what you can afford. Depending on the state of the housing market, there are times when selling your house may not be the best choice. If you cannot buy a home that fits your needs for the amount you will get from the sale of your house, then selling the house may not be the best choice. If selling the house means you will have to move into a different school district, move far away from your friends, or move into an area that is not safe, you may want to look at other alternatives before deciding to move. Your CPA, attorney, or financial planner may be able to help you in finding alternatives.

Alternatives to Moving

If you determine your finances are such that you cannot continue to pay the mortgage, there are alternatives you can consider.

1. If you have a good job, talk to your lender about refinancing. Refinance to reduce your monthly payment with a lower rate, even if you lengthen the time. This may allow you to remain in the house and get the payments in range for your budget. Be cautious when refinancing. Always have the terms and paperwork reviewed before making a decision to refinance.

2. Consider finding a second source of income. One possibility is taking on a second job, at least temporarily, to help while you are waiting for your income to increase on your main job. Some people have

taken in a roommate, which I discussed in Chapter 3.

3. Often people suggest that the logical answer is to take on a home job, such as selling cosmetics, or other party sales, or that sort of thing. Think carefully before you do this. These companies generally require an investment, and unless you are very, very good at sales, most people don't make a significant amount of money from this.

Most importantly, before you make any decision about moving or staying, get solid advice from your attorney and from your accountant. Look fearlessly at your finances and at what you need emotionally. Only then can you determine what is best for you and your family. Remember that well-meaning advice from other people is just that – well-meaning, but they are not living your life and do not know what your needs are. Take time to breathe, get all the facts, and make the decision that is best for you and your family.

CHAPTER VII

Old Friends, New Friends

Finding Where You Belong

> You need to love yourself enough that you can establish strong, healthy friendships in this new phase of life.

As you begin making new friends, you need to provide yourself with time and patience. You will not develop new friendships overnight.

MY STORY

After the death of my husband, I continued to socialize with old friends who had known the two of us and continued to accept me as part of the group. About eighteen months later, the church where most of my close friends were was closed and I found myself no longer in the constant company of people who knew and cared for me and my husband. I moved rapidly into a different church and made a shocking discovery. It's very hard for a single woman to find her place in a new social group.

I was a woman in my late forties, a widow with an elementary-age child. Most of the parents of children my son's age were substantially younger than I was. Most of the widows were past retirement age, and their children were grown. Those who were in my age group were couples. It was difficult to find a place to fit in the church. People were certainly polite and nice to me, but, while the couples who had moved into the church at the same time found friends to socialize with, I found it hard to make those connections.

Possibly one of the most startling events was when I was introduced to a man who had a pickup truck. I was asked to coordinate the movement of donated goods for a group I had been involved in. When we were introduced, the gentleman making the introduction looked at me and jokingly said, "You probably are not used to being hooked up with strange men," or some comment to that effect. The wife of the man with the truck then looped herself around her husband and said, "He's not very strange, but he is mine." It was clear from her attitude and body language that she was concerned about this single woman doing any activity with her husband.

FINDING WHERE YOU BELONG IS A NEW CHALLENGE

Old friends continued to stay friends, but increasingly you will find yourself not included in events that are couple oriented. Several factors are involved.

During group activities, men tend to spend time with men, and women spend time with women. Where there are large group gatherings, you will probably be included, but there will not be many invitations to activities with small groups of couples after the initial period of grief and support are passed. You may find yourself the "fifth wheel" in groups made up of couples.

If you have a small child, it becomes even more challenging to find where you fit.

When moving into new organizations and new groups, you have to look for an intentionally cultivated peer group. This can be extremely difficult when you are deep in grief and do not have the emotional energy to cultivate new friendships. If there is a grief group that has people of your age and your situation, it is a good place to start. If you are in a church, or social organization that has any kind of group comprised predominately of widows in your age group, that is often a place to begin to establish new friendships. You should look for an individual in your new group that is similarly situated and cultivate a relationship with her.

Another option is to find an activity that you enjoy which allows you to interact with people socially in a formal environment. When taking a class you have something in common with the other students. Teaching a Sunday school class allows you to interact with both the children and parents in a children's class or with adult students and other teachers. Choosing to serve on the board of a local charity or work in the local food pantry will bring you in contact with new people. All of these activities will broaden your social contacts and will allow you to become acquainted with and develop friendships with different people. By providing you with an opportunity to interact with people on a one-on-one basis, these friendships are formed without the necessity of connecting with both spouses. This provides you the opportunity to establish yourself as an independent person.

I frequently hear of women who have left their church, often the church where they grew up, were married, had their children, because it is now too hard to attend. The memories of a lifetime spent with their husbands in that church makes it too painful to ever return to the church. I would caution you against leaving a church or other organization because of the painful memories. Initially, everything you see will remind you of your husband and everything will make you cry. At times the pain seems unbearable.

The decision to cut your ties with old friends must be done with caution. Rather than abandoning your lifetime friends, I advise you to take occasional breaks. Go out of town for a weekend. Go see family. Go to church with another family member or friend. Skip a meeting of your organization. Allow yourself time to heal and to breathe.

Don't make a decision about leaving an organization for at least a year after death. You simply are not able to making rational decisions. When you choose to leave an organization and the people who are there, you leave yourself vulnerable and alone. Often, you cut yourself off from your support system. Re-establishing friendships as a single woman is much more difficult than staying with the people who already know you, love you, and will support you.

If you choose to begin again, remember that you are no longer part of a couple. You will not be the person invited to go to dinner with other couples. Couples tend to go with couples. While you continued to be included in couple's activities that you and your husband were a part of, you will probably not be included in couple's activities in the new organization. This does not imply that people intentionally don't want to be friends with you because you are single, or that they don't like you because you are single. It is simply the way things are. Couples tend to attract other couples. It gives some level of balance. It prevents the "fifth wheel" effect.

As you begin making new friends, you need to provide yourself with time and patience. You will not develop new friendships overnight. Remember that at this point in your life, you are very sad and probably not the best person to get to know. I was not a fun person in the first two or three years after my husband's death. While lifetime friends can tolerate hearing the story of your husband's death over and over and over, a process often necessary for you to deal with the death, people who don't know you well, and didn't know your husband, will often grow impatient with this and simply move on to someone more cheerful. So this requires you to strike a delicate balance between being morose and depressing (a very natural consequence of having lost a spouse) and forced gaiety, which will not encourage anybody to spend time with you.

While keeping yourself in touch with other human beings, don't neglect your family. Brothers and sisters can provide an enormous amount of emotional support. Occasional outings with them can be a big boost to your morale and help you to maintain a positive outlook on your social situation.

Don't overlook your in-laws. If you had a good relationship with your in-laws before your husband's death, allow them to step in and be your friends now. As time goes on, you may very well see less of them, but in the time immediately following the death, allow them to continue to be your friends. This is a time when you need friends.

Remember that adult children, while they can continue to provide support for you, will also be grieving (as will your in-laws), and will comfort you when they can. They are having to deal with the loss of a parent in their own way. Minor children should never be the sounding board for your grief. Discussing your grief with them and allowing them to express their grief is a normal and necessary part of grieving. However, they should never be used to provide you with the emotional support and friendship that you need. This is not to say that your children are not your friends, but your job is to support them, not theirs to support you.

DATING

As you step out and discover where you belong, be careful. There are many people who will claim to be your friend, but are not. Immediately after my husband's death, I began getting dating service calls. How they knew I was suddenly widowed, and how I got on the call lists, I don't know. Everybody wanted to help me find a new spouse. Friends tried to set me up (usually new friends, the old ones knew better) and offered to help me find a new husband. This began within months of my husband's death. I wasn't even fully conscious yet, and people felt like I should be moving on. Good friends, close friends, who knew you and your husband are not as likely to try to set you up immediately (which is not to say they won't try to set you up later).

Be cautious of blind dates. There are many people out there who are simply looking for a woman to utilize for their own purposes, whether that is sex, money, or a live-in housekeeper. Be inherently suspicious of strangers who discover you are a widow and befriend you. In my law practice, I have seen a number of cases of widows or widowers who were befriended at the hospital while their spouse lay dying. Subsequently, that person moved in with them and took them for everything they had, leaving the widow/widower not only alone, but penniless and sometimes homeless and deeply in debt. Be cautious in establishing new friendships with convenient strangers.

Don't be afraid of everyone, but use good judgment. If you're unsure about a person, consult with a family member you trust. Describe the situation openly and honestly, not defensively, and see if they see any red flags. As much as you want not to be alone, it is worse to be with the wrong person than to be by yourself. You have to love yourself enough that you will not allow yourself to be abused. You need to love yourself enough that you can establish strong, healthy friendships in this new phase of life. You also need to know that it is okay to be alone, okay to be a strong independent woman with friends and family who love and support her. Then, when you are comfortable with yourself, and your situation, it may be time to consider dating and establishing lasting relationships.

CHAPTER VIII

Grief, Guilt, and the Long Journey Back to Life

> The "what ifs" are not helpful. You cannot see an alternate future, a future that doesn't and cannot exist.

Guilt and grief are companions on our journey. Each produces its own set of challenges for the new widow.

MY STORY

When my husband (Bob) died, the death was sudden and unexpected. He had been healthy that morning, when he left the house. He and my nine-year-old son had gone camping at the local state park as a birthday celebration for my son, who was to turn ten on Monday. Bob had taken that Friday off from work, and they had been swimming, riding bicycles, hiking through the woods, had eaten a couple of hot dogs for dinner, and were waiting on a friend to come with his boat. As they sat at the campsite making plans to go camping in Colorado for spring break, Bob made a choking noise, put his hand on his chest, his head fell forward, and he was dead. My nine-year-old son called me.

As I explained in Chapter 1, I called for an ambulance, but it was all too late. In an instant, my life changed and I was plunged into grief.

AN OCEAN OF GRIEF

Over the next months and years, I came to describe grief as an ocean. One day you are walking along, life is normal, happy, and you are on the dry land. Suddenly you find yourself dropped in the middle of the ocean. The death of your spouse has turned your world upside down. You feel like you are drowning in grief. When you finally claw your way to the surface, you look around you, confused and dazed. You don't know where you are, and you don't know which direction the land is. You are in the middle of the ocean of grief and you can see no land in sight.

The sense is that there is no hope; that there is no way to recover from the grief. During the time immediately after death, you can expect yourself to be virtually non-functional.

Initially, after my husband's death, I described myself as being on auto pilot; completely numb and doing things without a lot of conscious thought. That got me through the few days between the death and the funeral. It was only afterwards, that I struggled to the surface of the water and looked around.

During the weeks that followed, I was simply treading water. I got up and did the things I had to do, but I was so overwhelmed by sadness that it was nearly impossible to focus on anything for more than a few minutes. My work did not suffer as badly as other parts of my life, because my work life was separate and distinct from my family life. At home I got food on the table, did laundry, and cried a lot.

THE FIRST FEW WEEKS

During the initial weeks, the pain of grief was so acute that I could feel it physically. It was a struggle to get out of bed, a struggle to feed my child, a struggle to remember to do daily tasks I needed to keep my family afloat. Once the initial numbness and auto pilot stage had passed, I found it essential to write notes to myself. Sometimes I posted sticky notes on my mirror in the bathroom. I found myself getting out of the house without brushing my hair, leaving the house with a suit jacket that didn't match my skirt, and getting to work one day in my bedroom slippers (I promptly put a pair of dress shoes at the office, so this couldn't happen again!).

Each day presented a new and difficult challenge during the time period of intense, all-consuming grief.

AFTER THE NUMBNESS

Eventually, you will find, as you tread water in the ocean of grief, that you pick a direction and begin swimming. You have awakened enough to realize you can't just stay out there and drown.

During the swimming phase, you work at pulling yourself together. Now you are more alert. The grief is less new and less painful. This stage often seems to occur several months after death. You begin doing routine things again, such as getting up and going out to eat. While you may not feel enthusiastic or energetic, you manage to do the things you need to.

SWIMMING IN THE OCEAN OF GRIEF

My husband died in August, and I was in the beginning of the swimming stage when the holidays rolled around. I know from talking to my family that I spent Christmas at my sister-in-law's, yet I have no recollection of Thanksgiving or Christmas that year. I don't really know who I spent them with, but I know I bought Christmas presents for everyone, made lists, and did the things I was supposed to. I even got a Christmas tree put up.

At some point, you pick a direction and begin the long swim back. You are swimming, and swimming, and, eventually, you reach the shore. You see dry land. You crawl onto it, and before you open your mouth to say, "I've made it!" you get washed back into the ocean of grief by a giant wave. "Reaching shore" is the first time you realize you are not actively thinking about being sad. You have a brief moment where you are happy and peaceful and calm. Something has allowed you to forget your grief, and the very recognition that you are not sad plunges you back into your sadness, and you begin the process over again.

As I've talked to widows in my practice, I've described grief this way: the ocean, the swimming, the crawling on land. Most recognize the description. Eventually, you will find that you are on land for longer and longer periods of time before you are swept back in the ocean. Finally, one day, you realize you are on land more than in the ocean, and the grief begins to abate. This can take months or even years. For me, it was several years. Don't let people tell you it will happen overnight. It happens to each person in her own time, and it is dependent on many factors, including how long you and your husband were together. So be prepared for a long journey back to life.

Thomas remembers ...

I can never seem to wrap my head around the reason behind my dad's departure. I wanted to blame someone, but there was no one to blame. I knew at the time he died of natural causes. That's what the doctors say. It never seems to help though. They always seem to think that saying, "Oh, he passed away peacefully" helps. It doesn't!

IF ONLY I HAD ...

Guilt is an interesting factor in grief. For many of us, there is the opportunity to look back and say, "If only I had done this. If only I had done that. Why didn't I kiss him goodbye that morning? Why was I angry when he left? Why wasn't I better to the person who's died?" My brief stint with guilt came in the fact that my husband had repeatedly called me the day he died, and during the last call had asked me if I wanted to come out and join them for hot dogs for dinner. He laughed when he asked, because he knew I would say no; but he always asked.

Needless to say, I said no. I was looking forward to my evening alone. I didn't realize it would be a lifetime alone.

After his death, I felt guilt for not having gone out to eat with them. My brain just played the "what if" game. "What if you had gone to eat hot dogs? You might have been there when he collapsed. What if you had been there? Could you have kept him alive until the paramedics got there? Would the outcome have been different?" What if? What if? What if?

The "what ifs" are not helpful. You cannot see an alternate future, a future that doesn't and cannot exist. As much as you'd like to, you cannot change what happened, so you have to accept the past for what it is and acknowledge your new future.

I encourage you to get professional help if the guilt is overwhelming you, and to recognize it for what it is. It's part of the grief process, but it's a learning process. If your treatment of the person who has died left you feeling guilty, then you have an opportunity to learn how to treat those around you whom you love and who are still alive.

My advice to my son is, when you are married, never go to sleep without speaking. Never go to sleep without saying "I love you." Never leave the house without saying "I love you."

The morning of Bob's death, he asked me to go eat breakfast with the two of them. I almost said no. I was busy. I had work to get to the office, and I wasn't sure I had time to eat breakfast. He offered to go to Braum's, which would be relatively fast, and I decided being twenty or thirty minutes late to work, to have breakfast with "my boys," was a good trade-off. Looking back, I have forever been grateful that I did. I certainly dodged a "guilt bullet" at that point, and I have a memory of the last breakfast with my husband and my son, the last meal together as a family, a happy one. As I got up to leave, Bob followed me out to the car and kissed me goodbye and told me he loved me. Never say goodbye without saying "I love you."

As you deal with guilt, remember that you could not have known how that day would end. If you had known how, you might have done things differently. Even if you didn't do something to feel guilty about, your brain may invent something. Do not be afraid to get professional help if you need it.

As you deal with grief, you must stop focusing on the "what ifs" and focus on "what's next."

CHAPTER IX

Children of All Ages

Helping Them Help You

> Remember that the child is going through all of the same emotions that you are: disbelief, sadness, guilt, anger, and you need to help the child find a suitable way of expressing them.

Your children, whether age 2 or 42, are grieving. In their grief they need their mother. In spite of your own grief, you must help your children deal with their father's death.

<u>MY STORY</u>

Thomas was nine when his father died. He turned ten between the death and the funeral. It is a tough way to celebrate a birthday. Kids of all ages have fears and insecurities surrounding the death of a parent. They have many of the same emotions that we do, as well as some most adults don't experience; sometimes slower, sometimes much faster than the adults. You have to be willing to answer their questions openly and honestly, as hard as it is to do.

Bob died on a Friday night. On Saturday night, as I was up until the wee hours of the morning waiting for the arrival of out-of-state family, Thomas stayed up with me. When I finally walked him down the hall to go to bed, about 1:00 in the morning, assuring him that the relatives would be there the next morning, he looked at me and said, "Mom, about this new husband thing." I said, "Yes, dear, what about a new husband?" He looked at me, his eyes big and sad, "Are you going to get one right away?" Trying not to look startled, I assured him I was not going to remarry anytime soon. He sighed, looked relieved and said, "Good. I don't think I'm ready yet."

Thomas had seen so many revolving door marriages, that he assumed I would remarry immediately. Even in my grief, my pain, and my numbness, I had to laugh at the nine year old saying, "Good. I'm not sure I'm ready yet," little more than twenty-four hours after his father's death. Perhaps he thought you got new husbands off the shelf at the store.

CHILDREN AND GRIEF

Small children have different fears, and different reactions from older children. The very youngest children understand very little about death. They don't understand its permanence, and they don't understand what's happening. You need to take time to sit down and explain to them, in whatever fashion you choose, that their daddy is gone. "He has gone to live in Heaven," is often an explanation that is given. In Christianity, we often say, "He's gone to live with Jesus in Heaven." This does give children a sense that he is no longer here.

When dealing with children, they need to be reassured that:

1. <u>Their daddy loved them and didn't leave on purpose</u>. Children cannot be allowed to believe that their daddy went away because of something they did, or that he will be coming back. Often children believe that the person is gone because of their bad behavior, and will come back if they are better. The smallest children need to understand that their father still loved them, and his departure, his death, had nothing to do with the child. A story I remember reading in college told of a young child who seemed to be taking her father's death very stoically indeed. Calm and composed, the child never cried. Everyone commented on how well the little girl was handling her father's death. Then one day a visitor noticed the little girl putting an apple on the window ledge. When asked why, the girl told them that her daddy liked apples. She thought if he saw it in the window, he wouldn't be mad at her anymore and would come home.

This is often hard to deal with in the middle of your own grief, but children need to know, even at the youngest age, that the death is not their fault. At one point Thomas tried to blame himself for Bob's death, because they had been so active that day. Elementary-age children, such as my son, also need to be reassured frequently that it is not their fault. They need to be given an opportunity to discuss their sadness. Watch for changes in behavior, eating or sleep patterns. Not grieving at all can be an indication of trouble. If there is a concern, get professional help.

As with younger children, teens may also need the opportunity to talk about the parent, and the opportunity to grieve. I've seen parents who choose to try to keep their children happy all the time. It hurts to see them sad, but it also tells them that they should not be grieving for their father. Remember that the child is going through all of the same emotions that you are: disbelief, sadness, guilt, anger, and you need to help the child find a suitable way of expressing them.

2. <u>It is normal to be angry</u>. At one point, as my son rocketed through the grief process (much, much faster than his mother!), he was very angry. We were in the car driving on the freeway. (Why do kids always tell you things that require your full attention when you are flying down the highway at 65 m.p.h.?) He told me he was angry with God for letting his father die, but he thought that it was wrong to be angry with God. We talked a little about the fact that God understood how he felt, and that if he was angry with God, I felt like God could take it. God has big shoulders. God knew that Thomas loved Him and He loved Thomas and Thomas's dad, and God knew that he was hurting. Being angry with God is normal, but it is startling to hear a child say it. You need to stay calm, and not be shocked by the statement. Your child doesn't need any more guilt.

Several weeks later in the car (of course), he was really angry with me. "Where were you when I called?" he demanded. The first call had come when I was driving home from work, and two or three minutes later his second phone call came in, soon after I walked into the house. It was after that second call that I called for the paramedics. I looked at him quietly and said, "I was in the car coming home from work." He was silent and thoughtful for a few minutes, then sighed and said, "I guess that's all right then." He wanted to be angry with me. He wanted it to somehow be my fault. You must be prepared for the child to be angry with you and blame you for your husband's death. Just as you will get angry at God, at somebody, at the world, your child will also experience that same anger, and they need to be met with kindness, gentleness, and the recognition that the anger is a normal part of the grief process.

    3. <u>Children must be allowed to talk about their father.</u> My husband's father died when Bob was a teenager and I often heard Bob tell me that after his father's death, he was never spoken of again in the family. It was as if his dad had never been. The impression Bob had was that it was too hard on their mother to remember him, so he was just never mentioned. This deprived the children of the chance to grieve together with their mother, to acknowledge their loss, to have their feelings of sadness and emptiness and the loss validated. It was very detrimental to the older children not to have the chance to revere their father, to express their love and their sadness.

    With older children and teenagers, those who are sad, and those who are angry, it is important that they know their feelings are valid. While we recognize that their feelings are valid, that doesn't mean a teenager's misplaced anger isn't a problem. We have to help them find ways to work through the anger and grief and come out of it a stronger person.

A child I met, several years after Bob died, had lost his father around the same time. After that death, the family stopped doing things that had painful associations with the father. This allowed the child to withdraw and brood. When I met him, he had retreated into his room and did virtually nothing but school.

4. <u>Allow your children to grieve with you</u>. It is normal to want to keep your children busy and entertained. We want them to be happy. Many times we also want to avoid their sadness. It is simply too painful to see.

When my own father died many years ago, we were in the viewing room when the funeral director asked us to leave for a moment. They had something they had to do. When we came back in, the casket had been draped with the American flag. Bob, seeing the American flag, did something I had never seen him do. He burst into tears. We stood there in the viewing room holding each other and sobbing. It is a memory that will still make me cry, but there was something tremendously comforting about not being alone in my grief. Knowing that my grief was valid and knowing it was shared by somebody I loved was important to me.

Allowing your children to cry, and crying with them so they know they are not alone, painful as it is, can be beneficial. There are times when you need to grieve together and there are times when you need to be strong. There is nothing wrong with allowing the child to show that he misses his parent, that you miss your husband, that you all loved him. It tells the child you understand that your child feels all of the same things you do, only in a different way. Grieving together lets the child know it is okay to feel the loss, and that you understand that. It also allows the child to understand that it is okay to be sad, even when that makes mom sad, too.

5. <u>Watch for behavioral changes.</u> With minor children of any age, behavioral changes, evidence of problems in the grieving process, or any acting out behavior, should be seen by a child psychologist. The grief process is hard enough to handle as an adult. As a child, it is easy to interpret the action of the sad adults around you in an incorrect way. I encourage you to take your grieving children to see a psychologist who specializes in dealing with children and adolescents.

At the encouragement of many people, I took my son for three sessions with a psychologist, and the last session we spent together. The psychologist had me telling Thomas all the ways he was like his father. I thought that showed a great deal of understanding on the part of the psychologist. My child absorbed that information and came to understand that, though Bob was dead, a part of him lived on inside his son.

I have seen him grow into a strong, honest, reliable, wonderful, young man with many, many of Bob's best characteristics. The psychologist laid a foundation for that, but most of the foundation was put in place by the nine, nearly ten, years they spent together as a father and son. A psychologist can help a child, or a teenager, move through the steps of grief and get on with his or her life, which is a benefit, not only to them, but to you as a grieving parent.

6. <u>Allow your child to live in the moment.</u> On Thomas's 10th birthday, we had the viewing at the funeral home. Several hundred people packed into a relatively small space. Many of them wanted to pat, hug, or otherwise console my son. They all knew him, but he didn't know them. He responded with grace and dignity beyond his 10 years. However, when his 23 and 25-year old cousins offered to take him to a movie, I gratefully let him go. He was happy to spend part of his birthday going with his cousins to see a movie.

Children can be happy in the moment, even during times of intense grief. While I could not smile, laugh, enjoy a movie, or set aside my grief for even a moment during the first few weeks, Thomas could. Children can live in the moment, enjoying what is right at hand, without regretting the past or worrying about the future. It is a gift children have (and I would have given anything to have) and they should be allowed to have it. Enjoying themselves at a movie or party is not a lack of respect or failure to grieve. It is just how children are made. Allow them to live in the moment and allow the child to be joyful even in grief.

7. <u>Be prepared for your children to cling to you.</u> At 16, Thomas confessed to me that he was always a little afraid when he saw me leave him (at school, the movie theater, the airport) that he might never see me again. He had lost one parent and was afraid of losing another. It was a very reasonable feeling.

I was fortunate Thomas did not become clingy. I continued to encourage him to go on Scout campouts and sleepovers. As hard as that was <u>for me</u> the first few times, I was determined not to cause him to be aware of it.

Some children become so frightened, they refuse to leave their parents. Sometimes this is spontaneous, but sometimes the fear of separation comes from the mother. As mothers, if we are not careful, our grief is interpreted by the child as fear of another loss. Try to keep routines as normal as possible. If your child begins to exhibit signals of new or increased fear of leaving you, seek the assistance of a grief counselor or child psychologist.

Thomas remembers …

I've been told that many things are the hardest things in the world, but none of them can compare to growing up without a father. It has been the hardest and the longest journey I have ever embarked on. My mother was there for me every step of the way. I only got to know my father for 9 years and on my 10th birthday he left me and my mother all alone in this immense world.

At 10 years old I knew it had happened, but only wished that my father was only sleeping. He was sleeping, but it was an eternal rest. It was so hard not to break down every minute of every day during the months following my father's passing, but I knew I had to be strong. I had to be strong not only for myself, but also for my mother. She needed to know that I was all right.

Thomas Remembers, continued...

She had enough to deal with. She didn't need a depressed little boy on her hands, so I would always stand by her side and just talk to her. It's kind of interesting, for my mother felt the exact same way as I did. When this was revealed, we were really able to talk and enjoy each other's company.

The years went by and I realized how hard it is to grow up without a father.

Thomas Boyanton

ADULT CHILDREN

Adult children are a different matter. Children early in their careers, or in college, who are wrapped up in their own family life, college, the exploration of adulthood, will feel the impact, but will feel it less severely than you. This seeming lack of grief should not be taken as an indication of a child who did not love his/her parent, or an uncaring or unfeeling child. Children in their late teens and twenties are heavily involved in creating their own life, their own independence. It's an exciting time and, as sad as the death of a parent is, it usually only affects them on the peripheries of their lives. They are busy galloping into the future, starting jobs, getting married, having babies. Parents are part of the past. They are sad. They grieve, but the parent that's lost seldom impacts their daily life and daily routine the way it does the surviving spouse.

Those adult children, who are already settled, will frequently want to help and protect the parent who is left behind. A child may become overprotective of her mother, wanting you to call every time you leave and return to the house, and trying to take care of you as much as she would take care of a child. It's important that you allow her the opportunity to assist you. However, you need to determine how much and what type of help you need. Bear in mind that you need to decide what direction your life will take, but it can't be done for a number of months after death. As I've said before, I encourage you not to make life-changing decisions for at least a year. While you may not want your child to make decisions for you, allow your children to help you in ways that are <u>actually</u> helpful to you, and helpful to them.

In the initial months after death, taking over some of your husband's tasks at home may be appropriate for your adult children, like mowing your lawn, and helping make home repairs. Perhaps they could help you understand how to pay bills, budget, get your car inspected, or any things that you're not familiar with. Temporarily, let your children help you learn to do things you are not familiar with, so that you will not be permanently dependent on their help. Be careful here. Adult children, like other well-meaning relatives, will try to make decisions for you. Remember, you're sad, not incompetent, and can still make your own decisions.

HELPING ADULT CHILDREN GRIEVE

In addition to your children helping you, they will need your help. You are still their mother. They need to know that it's okay to talk about their Dad with you. Just as the mother of minor children doesn't want to upset them by talking about their dead father, so your adult children may want to not upset you and make you cry. They need to know that being sad is a normal part of the grief process, and that if talking about their Dad makes you cry, it is all right. Eventually you will be able to talk about him without crying. It's important that they be allowed to remember the good things, and be allowed to talk about them with the person who is now most important to them - you.

Children eventually find their own resolution to the process, just as you will. Adult children will usually get to the end of this road faster than you will, because, despite their love for the parent, and the fact that they miss their father, in most cases he was not involved in their daily lives. They have respite from grief as they go about their everyday affairs. For you, there is little respite. Your spouse was an intimate part of every aspect of life, and you miss him intensely. Children who are grown and out of the household do not grieve in the same way.

OUT OF THE MOUTHS OF BABES

Children do have a remarkable ability to recover. About a year after my husband's death, I was driving with Thomas on the freeway. While we were driving,

Thomas looked at me and said, "You know mom, we're lucky Dad died at the lake." I had a little trouble getting my head around the idea of "lucky." I kept thinking, "Lucky…lucky…lucky? How is any of this lucky?" So I turned, smiled at Thomas and said, "Oh, how so, dear?" "Well," Thomas began thoughtfully, "It would have been much worse if Dad had died at the bank. This way he got to spend his whole last day doing something he loved, and I got to spend his whole last day making him happy." How right Thomas was. How quickly he had dealt with the reality of death, and found the silver lining. I looked at him and thought, "Hang on to that for the rest of your life. It's true and it's good, and it's the best answer I've ever heard." Thomas has grown up to be a fine young man. He grew up without guilt, without being trapped in grief, knowing that he spent his Dad's last day making him happy.

CHAPTER X

Living With the Past and Running From the Past

Dealing With "Stuff"

A change of scenery, or a change of possessions around us, is not the answer or the cure for grief. The grief is inside of us, and while certainly a change may present a temporary respite, a distraction from our grief, the grief is inside each of us and will return, no matter where we are.

Possessions can take on a huge emotional significance after death. They can evoke tears and laughter. Deal with your husband's possessions when you are ready to.

<u>MY STORY</u>

In Chapter 2, I told you about my experience with opening a can of my husband's deodorant. Looking back, I have to laugh at my reaction. Even at the time, I recognized the humor in a 48-year-old woman, collapsed in a heap on the bathroom floor, sobbing and clutching a deodorant can. Sometimes in the midst of the overwhelming grief, you still have to see some of the humor in your situation.

After having such a strong reaction to the deodorant that I disliked, I decided not to deal with his clothes for a while. They weren't in my way and Thomas might want some of his Dad's clothes when he grew into them. Admittedly, he was ten at the time and it was going to be a long time before they fit him, but I put off dealing with the clothes for over a year.

WAIT A YEAR BEFORE DISPOSING OF ALL HIS "STUFF"

Well meaning people will try to help you in dealing with the property of your deceased spouse. Many of them feel it will be helpful if they came in, go through all of your husband's stuff, and carry it all away. Surely, they reason, it will be less painful for you not to have to see it all the time. For some people, the removal of the personal property seems like the easiest way to stop hurting. Looking around and seeing the things of everyday life still where they were before your husband's death can be extremely painful; however, as with everything else, I encourage you not to make life-changing decisions until you have had the opportunity to pass through the initial stages of grief.

Personal property, much of which has sentimental value, falls in that same category of life changing decisions. Once gone, items cannot be recovered, no matter how much you miss them. I generally encourage people not to dispose of most personal property for a year. However, obvious trash, such as empty deodorant containers, don't have sentimental value, and can be thrown away. Business papers that have been brought home may need to be returned to the office within days of the death. Things that clearly are not useful, and do not have an emotional attachment, can be disposed of.

In my case, my husband had purchased about two hundred old computers, computer monitors, and miscellaneous parts at a school district auction the year before he died. He had great plans for these computers. I, on the other hand, had absolutely no use for them. It was far less than a year when I began sorting through and disposing of all of those outdated, useless, computer parts.

MEMORIES VERSUS STUFF

The choice you face is whether you want to live with the memories and the stuff, or you want to dispose of the stuff. The urge to escape from the pain of a past that is lost to you is normal; however, you have to ask yourself if removing everything that reminds you of your husband will, in fact, make it less painful.

A change of scenery, or a change of possessions around us, is not the answer or the cure for grief. The grief is inside of us, and while certainly a change may present a temporary respite, a distraction from our grief, the grief is inside each of us and will return, no matter where we are.

RECONCILING MEMORIES AND GRIEF

In your own way, you have to determine how to live with your grief, and to live with your past. In time, you will come to recognize that the past holds joyful memories, not just the last memories of illness, death and grief. When that time comes, you will look at the photographs and the precious keepsakes, and with each one, you remember the good times in your life. If you have chosen to run from all those memories because of the pain, you will lose the tangible memory triggers that come with the items you associate closely with your husband.

I recently received a survey on the Internet. It was the kind of survey people consider fun and forward to you. This time it was a Christmas survey. It asked a whole litany of questions about what you like to eat, what your traditions were, etc. One of the questions was about how you like to decorate your Christmas tree; single color? multi-color? coordinated theme? or colored theme? As I looked at my choices, I had to write in a different choice, because my tree contains a "garage sale" effect of ornaments. As I walk around and look them over, I can see the heart shaped ornament made out of some kind of thin shell material, with Bob written on it in glitter. I bought it for him the first year we were married, when we didn't have enough money to buy expensive ornaments. I see the tiny wooden ornaments given to me as a child by a family friend who traveled to Germany. I hold a faded green ornament with my name in silver glitter that hung on the family tree as I grew up. There are bead-studded ornaments my grandmother made when I was a child. There are ornaments from vacations Bob and I took, ornaments he brought me from business trips, ornaments that celebrate anniversaries and births, ornaments that remind me of bad times in my life, as well as good ones.

One ornament was given to me by someone who later caused a serious problem in my life. People do not understand why I kept the ornament. Now as I look at the ornament on my tree, I realize that even when there are unpleasant events, good can come from them and we will survive. So, though the ornament does not reflect one of the joyous times in my life, it does show that perseverance allows us to go forward and survive, even times we think are difficult.

As you deal with personal property, as you make decisions about the "stuff" of ordinary life, deal with it gently. Disposing of everything at once is often a bad plan. If it is not in your way, there is no requirement that you do this immediately. You may dispose of the property in your own time and in your own way. It may take you several months or years to go through things. I found for me, that in the first few months, it was hard to do more than a little at a time, because it made me so sad.

You may find yourself clutching deodorant cans, jogging shorts, or the jacket he always wore to work. All of those things evoke memories, feelings and emotions, and can be hard to deal with. Some of them you will want to keep and some you will give away, but everyone does it in their own time.

TAKE CHARGE

Do not feel compelled to clean things out because your children, your relatives, or your friends want you to. If people offer you help and you are ready, accept the help and embrace it; but do not allow yourself to be pushed into doing something you are not ready to do. In the end, there will come a time when you can look at the

Christmas ornaments on the tree and smile. Like me, you will remember what it was like to buy the seashell ornament on your trip to the beach. You will look at the painting and remember buying it in Europe, from a street vendor who just painted it. You will be able to hold the favorite sweater you kept and remember fondly your husband wearing it, perhaps someday seeing it worn by your child.

Only you can determine what is important to you and what is not. <u>Do not</u> be pushed into doing things before you are ready. Don't dispose of everything immediately, because it may be a mistake you will regret later.

CHAPTER XI

Taking Out the Garbage, Fixing the Broken Door, And Other Miscellaneous Things You've Never Dealt With

> Never use a chainsaw alone. Always read the instructions and warnings before using yard equipment. Don't do your own electrical work. Get help when you need it.

Taking charge of all aspects of your life can be scary. You may be surprised at what you can do when you have to!

MY STORY

Bob had many, many, many good attributes. He was a kind, generous man who was supportive of me in every aspect of me in my life. He was a wonderful husband, and a really devoted father. He led our Cub Scout den, and the children and the parents loved him. He was the kind of person everybody wanted as their friend, and, in fact, everybody counted as their friend. He was dependable. He was chronically happy and always willing to help with a giant smile on his face.

Having said that, while he was doing everything for everyone else, our garage door was held together with bailing wire so it would close. There was no water in one sink in the bathroom, nor was there hot water in my son's bathroom. A broken door had been screwed to the floor, and one of the French doors was "repaired" with nails temporarily holding it together. There were spots on the ceiling that had been sealed with sealer, but the ceilings had not been repainted. The kitchen had one florescent light and one of the old original fixtures. One of the toilets was not fully attached to the floor. Throughout my home there were things that had been "temporarily repaired" and made to work, but were held together with duct tape and wire.

While that approach worked well during his lifetime, when he was here to continuously coax them into working, I was not able to rattle, jiggle or cajole them into working properly. Consequently, in the months and years that followed, I had to get a new tractor, new lawn mower, a new garage door, a new garage door opener, and all new appliances, as they systematically fell apart (I'm convinced they knew he had died and that I couldn't fix them, so they just self-destructed!) I had massive amounts of plumbing work done; extensive repairs, painting, roofing work, and most recently had all of my ductwork reworked and a new air conditioning system put in.

THINGS YOU NEVER HAD TO DO

So, how do you deal with the many things you have never done? First is to pay attention to them. Do not leave them to get worse simply because you don't know how to do it. Taking out the garbage and putting gas in your car are fairly easy ones. While you may be angry and resentful of having to do it all, you will adapt and do those kinds of things. However, some of the other things you are faced with after your husband's death may be more difficult. I once knew a woman who was very concerned about her financial position after her husband's death, so she completely re-roofed her house herself. I'm not in any condition to do roof work, so consequently, among the things I had to have done after my husband died was an entire new roof.

PAYING BILLS

One of the things that I see in my practice is women who simply do not know how to pay bills. They have never paid any bills. Their husband always did. Often I have to sit down with a new widow, review her monthly bills, and teach her how to read each bill. I help her set up a system to pay the bills on time each month. While this sounds like a fairly simple thing, it's not an activity she is familiar with, and she needs to develop a specific habit of paying bills on time. In my office, we teach new widows how to do that. We provide an organizational structure.

For many women, the first thing is to set aside an area in which all bills are placed as they arrive. For those who need it, we set up the process:

1. Open the bill, read the bill, determine when it is due, and note that information on the outside of the envelope.

2. Place it in your bill holding area.

3. <u>Set aside a specific day or two of the month to pay bills.</u> If you are paid more than once a month, you may want to set up two payment dates.

When you are looking at bills, you must be cautious to ensure that you get them paid on time. Late fees and overdraft fees are expensive. If a bill falls due in the middle of the month and you need to pay bills at the first of the month, you must ensure that you have the bill in time to pay on the first of the month. Trying to wait until it comes in later in the month will almost ensure that the money will be gone and you will not be able to pay it in a timely fashion.

For many women, using a bill-paying calendar is helpful. On that bill-paying calendar, they note the date that specific bills generally arrive and when they are due. That way, when a bill is missing they can track it.

Paying bills online has become more and more attractive. Bill paying online allows you to schedule your payment for any day of the month, thus insuring that the payment is made on time. Setting up online bill pay or direct pay for set amounts can be very beneficial. I encourage widows who are unsure about bill paying to set up direct pay or automatic online payments for things that are essential, and cannot afford to be missed, such as mortgage payments, car payments, and insurance payments. I generally do not encourage automatic payments on credit card payments, because of the varying nature of the amount and the uncertainty as to whether there will be sufficient assets to cover it. Find a system that works for you to allow you to keep track of the bills, and to pay them on a regular basis. Whichever system you choose to use, be sure and log payments into your checkbook so you won't overdraw your account.

HOME REPAIRS

Home repairs are a new area for many women. First, I would advise you to get a good general home repair book. Go to any home improvement store, and ask someone to recommend a book. Tell them that you need a very simple book that gives you directions for simple repairs, such as replacing glass in a window (I've had one that has been out several months and I can't seem to get it replaced), replacing a doorknob, attaching towel bars and toilet paper holders, and other simple repairs around the house. Once you have this book, don't be afraid to try it. Try making simple repairs yourself. You may be surprised at how much you can do.

More complex repairs, repairs that require more physical strength than you have, or repairs that involve either plumbing or electrical work probably should not be undertaken by an amateur. In those cases, you need to find a competent, honest plumber, electrician, and handyman in your area. To find someone, begin talking to other people you know, both male and female, and ask if they use someone that they trust and believe would be a good person for you to use. Don't hesitate to talk with the repair people, interview them on the phone, find out how they charge for their services, and how quickly they can come. These kinds of questions are essential to determine whether they are suitable for you. Always ask if their employees are bonded and licensed. Make sure your electrician or plumber is licensed by your state, and that they are bonded. Handyman services may or may not be bonded, depending on what type of work they do.

Many women can do their own yard work, depending on the size of the yard. Learning to start the tractor or the lawnmower may be a challenge, if you have never used them. If the equipment is old, you may need to buy a newer model with an easier starter. We have gone from a pull start to a key start, because my arthritis makes a pull start hard for me.

Always read the instructions and warnings before using any yard equipment. Be especially cautious if you choose to use chain saws or other power trimming, sawing, or edging appliances. If you are unfamiliar with these, get instructions from someone familiar with the equipment before they are used. Never use chainsaws or power saws alone. Always have someone else with you in case of an accident.

Remember that there are many things you can do, or that you can learn to do. There are also things that you can't do, or learn to do, and for those you can hire someone. Sometimes hiring someone is a better choice than waiting on family to try to assist you. When you hire someone, you can get things done on your own timetable and on your own terms.

CHAPTER XII

Loving Yourself

It Just Takes Time

Weeping endures for the night, but joy comes in the morning.

Some of this is repeated from other chapters, but it is so important to understand what is happening to you. Only then can you wait patiently, loving yourself, until joy comes again.

MY STORY

It's been nine years since my husband's death, and life feels relatively normal again. I've learned to function by myself, and recognize that I will survive. I've gone through the anger, the guilt, the immense sadness, and the years of walking around in a trance. I recall the exact moment when I knew I was waking up. I was driving in the car, on the way home from work, driving down a street lined with trees just putting out spring leaves, the sky was bright blue, and signs of spring unfolding around me, and I realized, suddenly, that I was smiling. Not smiling at something in particular, just smiling for no apparent reason. It came as a shock when I realized that it had been nearly five years since I had smiled for no reason. Gradually, as a person waking

110

from sleep, I have awakened from my long walk and become whole and joyful again.

OCEAN OF GRIEF

As I've said earlier, grieving is like being dumped in the ocean, and at first, you believe you are going to drown. You are under the water and you don't know which way is up, or which way is down, and you are struggling. You struggle even to catch your breath. Finally, your head pops above the surface of the water and you gasp for air. You discover that even though you're no longer drowning in your grief, and are aware the world still exists, you don't know which direction dry land is. Eventually, you start swimming in the direction you believe the land is.

I did not know, until my husband died, that grief produced such massive, physical pain. I had been through a number of deaths that had made me sad and impacted my life, but nothing like the death of my husband. The grief was physically painful for weeks.

TREADING WATER

Once the acute physical pain, the continuous crying, and the inability to do anything but cry, had passed, I described myself as being numb. I think the numb stage is like treading water. You are just working as hard as you can to stay right where you are and not sink back into the mire of sadness. At this point, in addition to being surrounded by friends, which you were during the early stage, you need to go through the motions of all of the normal things of life. You go to work. You go to children's soccer games. You go to Christmas celebrations, even though you don't want to, or you have Christmas dinner, even though you don't want to. If your tradition dictates that you host the family dinner every year, I suggest that you get help with it this year. The first year is hard. During the first year it's nearly always treading water. You know that the holidays will be hard, as all of the first events are. You go through the motions and get them behind you.

Sometimes unexpected events will catapult you out of your numbness. That happened for me when, a month after my husband died, America experienced the horrible events of September 11, 2001. My grief was dimmed as I mourned with the country for our collective losses. But, my grief was not gone, merely postponed.

SWIMMING AND LANDING

I can remember when I began swimming. I thought, "Hmmm, I am awake now. I've pulled out of my grief." Of course I was mistaken, you understand, but I was swimming hard toward the shore. I had begun to feel like I had perked up and was getting my life under control. As I moved toward the shore of grief, away from the ocean, I thought I had made it. I remember waking up one day, and as I was doing something I suddenly realized I seemed happy. As soon as I realized it, it was gone. I was plunged back into this whole process again. You need to be ready for the process to start over several times. The different phases are shorter, but it seems to come in giant waves, waves of grief. Be patient with yourself during each wave, and recognize that it's normal, and if you just love yourself and are kind to yourself, and everyone around you, it will pass.

As time went on, I found myself feeling more normal and happier for longer periods of time, and less covered by sadness; however, each time I thought I had turned the corner and I was "normal" again, I was wrong. I was still walking around in some sort of daze. While I had prepared for the pain of the first year events and anniversaries, I was unaware that the second year anniversaries would come back and bite me. I knew that the first Christmas would bother me, but the second Christmas was, in every way, much harder than the first. I was so sad, I don't even remember where I celebrated that first Christmas. Be prepared for the second holidays to be as bad, if not worse, than the first holidays. By the second year, you are more aware of your loss and feel it deeply.

TAKING CARE OF YOURSELF

During all this, as the grieving process progresses, you need to be kind to yourself. You need to love yourself and take good care of yourself physically. This means making sure you take any medications you are supposed to on a regular basis. This means getting to your doctor for your annual physicals. It means paying attention to changes that occur.

Eight months after my husband died, I had to have a hysterectomy. I had suddenly developed a sense of fullness and pressure in my abdomen, and my waist had gotten bigger. I went to my doctor who ordered a sonogram, mostly to provide me with peace of mind because of my recent loss. Unfortunately, what it provided me with was surgery because it showed some kind of mass on my ovary, and I ended up having a full hysterectomy. If I had not paid attention, if I had allowed myself to be so involved in the grief that I had not listened to my body, I might very well have missed a signal that may have saved my life.

It's good to make your medical practitioners aware of your situation, so that they will understand your situation when you consult them. I am fortunate in that all of my doctors are very skilled, compassionate, and attentive. They always took me seriously, even in a time when I was emotionally distraught and difficult to deal with. It is important that you have a good relationship with doctors who will watch for problems when you may not be able to see them yourself.

If you are having difficulty sleeping, are crying uncontrollably, or having severe depression, get medical assistance. There is nothing wrong with getting help. Grief is real! Sleeping is important. If you cannot sleep, you will not be able to deal with the things that you are faced with. If you cannot stop crying long enough to work, you are going to create other problems. Do what you need to do, talk with your doctor, and get help that you need to get through the immediate crisis.

TAKE TIME FOR YOURSELF

Take time for yourself. Take time to do things that you like and that make you feel good. Whether that is playing racquetball, jogging, taking a bath, getting a massage, doing scrapbooking, or taking a class, do something that makes you feel good about yourself.

It is important that you feel good about yourself. Get up every day and get dressed. Put on your makeup, and make sure your hair is clean and brushed. Taking care of yourself means recognizing that you still deserve to be taken care of, to look nice and feel good. Taking time for yourself acknowledges that.

FLYING SOLO

One of the issues that occurs after the death of a husband, is that you have to redefine yourself as an individual. This may mean going back to school, reentering the work force, or simply finding who you are as a woman alone, as opposed to who you are as half of a couple. It is important that, even though you are distressed, you continue to keep your appearance up as best you can. If you wear makeup, continue to put it on, even if it's a struggle. The temptation to stay in bed and not bother to get dressed has to be avoided. Get up every morning and do your morning routine. Shower, put on your makeup, and get dressed for the day. Even if you do nothing else, you will feel better about yourself if you are out of bed and dressed every day.

Don't feel pressured by friends to do things you don't want to do. Well-meaning friends may try to get you to go out with them to the local bar, club, or party, believing that it will somehow snap you out of your grief and miraculously make you happy again. They mean well. They truly want to see you happy again. But dating is an issue that must be engaged in on your own time schedule. It should not be done to appease your friends.

I encourage you to stay active and continue to do things that interest you. Diving directly into the dating scene is often a bad idea. Most people are vulnerable and unsure of who they are as individuals, especially after a long marriage, and don't know what they want at this point in their life. You need to be sure of who you are as an individual before you begin dating again. Bear in mind that many people will expect you to have "recovered" from your grief within six months or so after your husband's death, which is not sufficient time. You did not become who you are overnight, and you will not change overnight.

I remember in the movie <u>Yours, Mine, and Ours,</u> a friend of the father in the story saying to him that it had been a year since his wife's death and it was time he got back into the dating scene. This kind of well-meaning advice is common. People will offer to set you up with a man they know who has never married, or is recently divorced, or widowed. If you are not ready to date, simply tell them you are not ready. Tell them that you appreciate their help and will call when you are ready to begin dating. Do not allow yourself to be pressured into doing any kind of social activity that you are not ready for or interested in.

SHARING YOUR GRIEF

If you have minor children at home, you can love yourself by loving your children. In the early stages, allowing them to grieve and grieving with them, even crying with them is a very comforting experience.

I held Thomas when he cried. Often we cried together as I held him and he patted me. There was tremendous comfort in having my grief validated, knowing that I wasn't alone, knowing that it was all right to be sad. The sharing of grief was a gift he gave me. Giving that gift to your children, especially young children at home with you, allows them to know that it is all right for them to be sad, even if it makes you sad. It is a huge gift, not only to them, but also to yourself. Allow your children to talk about their Dad, and talk about him with them. Remember his good qualities over and over again, so they will never forget them. You will never forget them. Grieve together and heal together, but be aware that children heal much faster than we do, they live in the moment, and you have to allow that.

You must recognize that children live in the moment. The death is sad, but right now I'm at a movie, and the movie is funny. As adults, we can't live in the moment quite as well. We live in the past, in the present, and in the future. Remembering all the things we had, grieving over the things we don't have, looking at the future and wondering how we will survive keeps us from enjoying the present. We could all learn from children. Even while they are sad, they still laugh at a movie. Don't be angry when your children sit in front of the television and laugh. It's not because they did not love their dad, or because they don't miss him. It's because they have the ability to live in the moment.

For the entire first three years after my husband died, the only thing I would allow my son to watch, if I had to watch with him, were funny movies. There are five or six tapes that we can both do from memory now. Though I couldn't live in the moment, I knew that I needed to smile. I knew that I needed to laugh. Laughter is healing. I refused to watch anything that made me cry. I had cried enough. I refused to watch things that made me anxious. I was anxious enough. But, I needed to laugh. I needed to learn to live in the moment. So we watched these movies over and over again, because at least they made me smile.

Now, we have a series of on-going jokes. One of the moves we watched over and over was Muppets Classic Tales. It included the story of the little boy who cried wolf, and there is a line in it where somebody says to the wolf, "Look behind you. There is a really big sheep." The wolf says, "What do you mean by really big sheep?" At that point, the really big sheep sits on him, and he says "Oh, really big sheep!" As my son and I have traveled together to different places in the world, we have come across sheep in a field, and one of us will look at the other one and say, "Really big sheep!" and we will both laugh. It is an odd bond we will have for life.

Both laughing and crying together, talking about the past and future, will give you a bond that will take you much further than you would have believed possible. It is a bond between you and your child that will sustain you during trying times. Loving your child is loving yourself.

Thomas remembers ...

It's been almost ten years since he left me. There is not a day that passes by where I do not think of his return, even though it cannot be. I was not the only one, however, who had been affected by this abrupt departure. My mother, who had stood by him for all the years, expected to do so for many years to come. She took his death extremely hard.

My dad was an honest man who never tried to cheat anyone. He was always smiling. At least that's what all 1,000 people said who came to say goodbye. They all seemed to think that they were his best friend. The man was an amazing person.

BE PREPARED FOR UNEXPECTED REACTIONS

The Sunday morning after Bob's death, I woke up early and realized I had a houseful of relatives and no breakfast food. While everyone slept, I headed to the donut shop - hair still wet from being washed. Our church always had donuts before the service (Bob bought them every week) but I was early enough not to meet any of the members at the shop.

As I ordered the donuts, the unexpected happened. I started to sob. Bob always bought the donuts, but I was never with him, so I hadn't expected the reaction. As I sobbed, other customers began inching away from me, looking very concerned. I paid for my donuts and ran from the store.

A year later, early on a hot Saturday morning, with my hair wet, I ran into the donut shop to pick up donuts. The combination of the early morning, hot weather, wet hair, and the smell of donuts triggered a repeat of my performance of a year earlier. I was shocked by this reaction!

You need to know that unexpected events will trigger a grief reaction. Sights, smells, and sounds can all produce reactions that are unexpected. As time passes, these events will become less frequent and less severe. Eventually they will all but disappear and you will be able to go places without the fear of falling apart. It feels great when that happens.

And, yes, I can go to the donut shop again.

YOU WILL SURVIVE

In the end, you will survive. How you survive is largely your own choice, but you will survive the loss of a spouse, though it seems impossible at the time. Trust in yourself. Trust in God. Love yourself. Care for yourself. Be flexible enough to ask for help when you need it, and be honest enough to know when you need it. If you take care of yourself and your family, you will be whole again. Give yourself time and be patient.

Joy will come.

Appendix A

Decision Making Worksheet

1. What are you trying to decide? Write a clear and concise explanation of the problem at hand. If you are unsure of the problem, write down the different aspects of it and then determine the main issue.

2. List all of the facts you need to make the decision. Look at the question and determine what facts, financial, personal, or otherwise, you need to make the decision. Some of these relevant facts will be positive, such as, "I can save $600.00 a month if I move into a retirement village." Some of them may be negative, such as "I will have to change churches and will not see my friends as often."

3. List the different possible courses of action and number them. Each possible choice should be listed individually.

> 1. I can stay where I am.
>
> 2. I can move to a retirement village.
>
> 3. I can move my granddaughter in with me.
>
> 4. I can move in with my son and daughter-in-law.

4. List the pros (good points) and cons (bad points) of each choice. The good and bad points can be based on your financial situation, emotional reaction, interactions with people, or anything that you have discovered in your fact-finding that will result from that particular choice. Each choice should be listed with the pros on the left, and the cons on the right.

Choice 1:

Pro   Con

Choice 2:

Pro   Con

Choice 3:

Pro   Con

Choice 4:

Pro   Con

5. For each choice, list the possible outcomes, what you would expect to happen. For each one, list why you would want to choose it, and why you would not.

Choice 1: Living at home

Alone and Alive

Choice 2: Move to a retirement village

Choice 3: Move my granddaughter in with me

Choice 4: Move in with my son and daughter-in-law

6. List the choice that gives you the best possible outcome.
This should be the action you plan to take.

Appendix B

Your Financial Checkup

Monthly Expenses -List each expense separately:

Expense   **Amount**

_____ $ _____

_____

_____

_____

_____

_____

_____

                                    TOTAL: $_____

Occasional or Emergency Expense: TOTAL: $_____

Credit Card Purchases Monthly   **TOTAL:** _____

Expenses Paid Less Than Monthly - Converted to Monthly

List each expense separately   **Monthly Amount**

_____ $ _____

_____ $ _____

_____ $ _____

       TOTAL: $ _____

GRAND TOTAL OF MONTHLY EXPENSES: **$** _____

Income

Monthly Income:

Social Security: _____ $ _____

Retirement: _____ $ _____

Income from Job: _____ $ _____

Income from Second Job: _____ $ _____

Other income (List sources individually): _____ $ _____

TOTAL MONTHLY INCOME $_____

Income Received Converted To Monthly
    Income Received Quarterly $_____

    Times 4 - Divided by 12 $_____

Annual Income $_____

    Divided by 12 $_____

Other Income Received Less Than Monthly Converted to Monthly $_____

    GRAND TOTAL MONTHLY INCOME $_____

TOTAL MONTHLY INCOME MINUS MONTHLY EXPENSES
$_____

If your expenses are greater than your monthly income, then you are going to have to either increase your income or decrease your expenses in order to continue to live in your current situation. If your income is greater than your expenses, you should plan to begin putting a percentage of the excess income away immediately to provide for emergencies.

Appendix C

Net Worth

Assets

CD's

_____$_____

_____$_____

Annuities

_____$_____

_____$_____

Stocks

_____$_____

_____$_____

Bonds

_____$_____

_____$_____

Liabilities

Home Mortgage

_____$_____

_____$_____

Credit Card (Balances Owed)

_____$_____

_____$_____

**Notes Owed to Banks and
Other Institutions**

_____$_____

_____$_____

**Notes Owed on Cars and
Other Vehicles**

_____$_____

_____$_____

Real Estate   **Student Loans**

_____$_____   _____$_____

_____$_____   _____$_____

Vehicles   **Any Other Debts Owed**

_____$_____   _____$_____

_____$_____   _____$_____

Other

_____$_____   _____$_____

TOTAL ASSETS $_____   TOTAL LIABILITIES $_____

        TOTAL ASSETS $_____

        MINUS TOTAL LIABILITIES $_____

                    NET WORTH $_____

This should reflect the total value of everything you own on the date the assessment is done.

Net Worth is the value of everything you own, minus the value that is owed. It shows how much your estate is worth, if everything were paid off.

Appendix D

Important Information For Your Family

The following is a copy of a booklet we provide to clients in my office that allows you to provide your family with all of the necessary information for an emergency. This information should be kept in one place, where it is easily accessible, so that in an emergency your family can find everything they need, without having to dig through your paperwork.

Booklet found starting on next page:

IMPORTANT INFORMATION

FOR MY FAMILY

compliments of

The Law Office of

Janet Shafer Boyanton, P.C.

211 Executive Way

DeSoto, Texas 75115

(972) 298-6111

(972) 298-6301 facsimile

My Personal Information

Full Name: _____

Maiden Name: _____

Other Names Ever Used: _____

Current Address: _____

City, State, Zip: _____

Prior Address: _____

City, State, Zip: _____

Phone Number: _____

Cell Number: _____

Social Security Number: _____

Veteran: Yes _____   No_____

    Branch of Service: _____

    Dates of Service: _____

    Discharge papers are located: _____

    Service Number: _____

Contacts

Family and Friends to Contact in Case of My Death or Disability

Name	**Relationship**	**Phone Number**
_____	Father_____	_____
_____	Mother_____	_____
_____	Brother_____	_____
_____	Sister_____	_____
_____	Child_____	_____
_____	Child_____	_____

Professional/Service Contacts to Notify:

Name	**Relationship**	**Phone Number**
_____	Clergy_____	_____
_____	Attorney_____	_____
_____	Employer_____	_____
_____	Accountant_____	_____
_____	Insurance Agent (Auto)_____	

_____ <u>Insurance Agent (Home)</u> _____

_____ <u>Insurance Agent (Life)</u> _____

_____ _____ _____

_____ _____ _____

_____ _____ _____

_____ _____ _____

Financial/Legal Affairs

My original will (not a copy) is located at:

_____

My Power of Attorney is:

    Name: _____

    Address: _____

    Phone: _____

My alternate Power of Attorney is:

    Name: _____

    Address: _____

    Phone: _____

Alone and Alive

My original Power of Attorney (not a copy) is located at:

_____

My financial accounts are located at the following
institutions:

<u>Type</u>	<u>Institution</u>	<u>Account No.</u>	<u>Contact Person</u>
<u>Checking</u>	_____	_____	_____
<u>Savings</u>	_____	_____	_____
<u>Savings</u>	_____	_____	_____
<u>Savings</u>	_____	_____	_____
<u>CD</u>	_____	_____	_____
<u>CD</u>	_____	_____	_____
<u>CD</u>	_____	_____	_____
<u>Investment</u>	_____	_____	_____
<u>Investment</u>	_____	_____	_____
<u>Safe Deposit</u>	_____	_____	_____
_____	_____	_____	_____
_____	_____	_____	_____

(Attach a copy of <u>recent bank statements</u>, so your family will find it much easier to track these down.)

Savings Bonds are stored:

_____

My Life Insurance Agent(s) are:

_____ Policy Number: _____

_____ Policy Number: _____

_____ Policy Number: _____

I have a pre-paid funeral or funeral insurance with:

_____

_____

My current obligations/debts are with the following institutions:

Type	**Institution**	**Account No.**	**Contact Person**
Mortgage	_____	_____	_____
Home Equity	_____	_____	_____
Auto Loan	_____	_____	_____

Alone and Alive

Unsecured Loan _____ _____ _____

Credit Card _____ _____ _____

Credit Card _____ _____ _____

Credit Card _____ _____ _____

_____ _____ _____ _____

_____ _____ _____ _____

_____ _____ _____ _____

Real Estate Information

Real Estate Owned:

Address: How Acquired   Value
                        (purchased, inherited, gift)

_____

_____

_____

_____

Health Care Information

Physicians, Therapists, etc.

Name	Relationship	Phone Number
_____	<u>Primary Care Physician</u>	_____
_____	_____	_____
_____	_____	_____
_____	_____	_____
_____	_____	_____
_____	_____	_____

I have health insurance with:

Name	Policy Number	Phone Number
_____	_____	_____
_____	_____	_____

My Medicare Number is:

_____

I have a supplemental health insurance policy with:

_____ Policy Number:_____

I have Long Term Care Insurance with:

_____ Policy Number:_____

My original Advanced Healthcare Directive ("Living Will") (not a copy) is located at:

_____

I have given a Medical Power of Attorney to:

Name: _____ Phone: _____

Address: _____ Cell: _____

Alternate:

Name: _____ Phone: _____

Address: _____ Cell: _____

My original Medical Power of Attorney (not a copy) is located at:

_____

I regularly take the following medications:

Name   **Dosage**

_____   _____

_____   _____

_____   _____

_____   _____

_____   _____

_____   _____

_____   _____

_____   _____

_____   _____

I have the following health conditions:

Condition   **Treating Doctor**

_____   _____

_____   _____

_____   _____

Alone and Alive

_____   _____

_____   _____

Other Information I Want You To Know:

_____

_____

_____

_____

_____

Personal Funeral Information

Name:

_____

I request the following at the time of my death.

____ I do not wish to have a funeral or memorial service.

____ I would like a funeral or memorial service as detailed below.

1. I would like the following Scriptures read.

_____   _____

_____   _____

_____   _____

2. I would like the following hymns sung.

_____

_____

_____

3. Do you have any stories of your life or faith that you would like to have shared at this service? (Use a separate sheet if necessary.)

_____

_____

_____

_____

_____

_____

_____

_____

1. Name(s) of preferred individual(s) to assist in arrangements (relative, friend, pastor, attorney):

Name:

_____

Address: _____ Phone: _____

Name:

_____

Address: _____ Phone: _____

2. Pastor to be called:

Name:

_____

Address: _____ Phone: _____

3. Funeral Home to be called:

Name:

_____

Address: _____ Phone: _____

Please check the following if it is your desire.

Treatment of my body:

_____ That my body be sent to such medical, social, or scientific center as will accept it. (It is my responsibility to choose the institution or up to those who make my final arrangements.)

_____ That my body be cremated

_____ That my body be buried

Veteran desiring burial at National Cemetery:

Yes _____   No _____

5. Organ Donation:

____ It is my wish to donate whatever organs/parts of organs that are useful to the living.

____ **Do Not** donate my organs.

6: Added Instructions:

_____

_____

_____

_____

_____

_____

_____

_____

_____

Information For My Probate Attorney

Full Name:

_____

Address:

_____

_____

County of Residence:

_____

Place of Birth:

_____

Date of Birth:

_____

Spouse's Name:

_____

Living? Yes ____ No ____ Date of Death _____

List all prior marriages, how they ended and the date:

Spouse Name   How Marriage Ended   Date Marriage Ended
(death, divorce)

_____   _____   _____

_____   _____   _____

_____   _____   _____

_____   _____   _____

Do you have a current will? Yes ___ No ___

Codicil (Amendment)? Yes ___ No ___

Where is it
kept?_____

Executor's Name: _____ Phone: _____

Address: _____ Cell: _____

Alternate Executor: _____ Phone: _____

Address: _____ Cell: _____

Children:

Name   Address   Birth date/Deceased Date

_____   _____   ____/_____

Alone and Alive

_____ _____ ____/____

_____ _____ ____/____

_____ _____ ____/____

_____ _____ ____/____

_____ _____ ____/____

_____ _____ ____/____

Siblings

Name	**Address**	**Birth date/Deceased Date**
_____	_____	____/____
_____	_____	____/____
_____	_____	____/____
_____	_____	____/____
_____	_____	____/____
_____	_____	____/____

Alone and Alive

Parents

Address	**Deceased** **(Y/N)**	**Date**
_____	_____	_____
_____	_____	_____

Death Certificate Information

Name:

_____

First   Middle   Last   Maiden

Social Security Number:

_____

Date of Birth: ___/____/____ Citizen of what Country:

_____

Birthplace:

_____

Armed Services Branch:

_____

___ Married ___ Never Married ____ Widowed
____Divorced

Alone and Alive

Usual residence:

_____

City   County   State   Country

Current Street Address:

_____

Street   City   State

Type of work done during working life (even if currently retired):_____

_____

Father's Name:

_____

Mother's Maiden Name: _____

Index